TO ALICE

FROM BRYAN

26th Feb. 1990

DESERT ORCHID

DESERT ORCHID

The Story of a Champion

JONATHAN POWELL

STANLEY PAUL

London   Sydney   Auckland   Johannesburg

Stanley Paul & Co. Ltd

An imprint of Century Hutchinson Ltd
62–65 Chandos Place, London WC2N 4NW

Century Hutchinson Australia (Pty) Ltd
89–91 Albion Street, Surry Hills, NSW 2010

Century Hutchinson New Zealand Limited
PO Box 40–086, Glenfield, Auckland 10

Century Hutchinson South Africa (Pty) Ltd
PO Box 337, Bergvlei 2012, South Africa

First published 1989
© Jonathan Powell 1989
Reprinted 1989 (twice)

Set in $11\frac{1}{2}/12\frac{1}{2}$ pt Bembo 270
Printed and bound in Great Britain by
Butler & Tanner Ltd, Frome and London

British Library Cataloguing in Publication Data
Powell, Jonathan, *1945–*
    Desert orchid: the true story of a champion.
    1. Steeple chasing horses
    I. Title
    798.4'5

ISBN 0 09 174240 4

PHOTO ACKNOWLEDGEMENTS

The publishers would like to thank the following photographers for allowing them to reproduce their photographs in this book: AllSport, pp. 62, 113; Kenneth Bright, pp. 8, 128/129 (sequence); *Daily Mail*, p. 59; Ed Byrne, pp. 84, 110, 114 (both); Tony Edenden, pp. 17, 18 (bottom), 51, 97; W. Everitt, pp. 34, 124 (middle); Mel Fordham, pp. 32, 46, 116, 118, 124 (top); Allan Glenwright, p. 85; *Guardian*, pp. 10 (bottom), 14 (bottom); David Hastings, p. 122 (bottom); Alan Johnson, pp. 13 (top), 88, 89, 104, 120, 123; Roger Lings, p. 107; Laurie Morton, p. 21; Stuart Newsham, p. 23; Paddock Studios, p. 66; Bernard Parkin, pp. 13 (bottom), 14 (top), 18 (top), 98, 122 (top); Charles Parkin, p. 39; *Racing Post*, pp. 98, 112 (bottom); W. W. Rouch, p. 108; Bill Selwyn, p. 111; George Selwyn, pp. 24, 27, 30, 31, 35, 36, 37 (bottom), 38, 41, 44/45, 46, 47 (three), 50, 53, 58, 60/61, 63 (bottom), 64/65, 67, 68, 69, 70, 71, 73, 74/75, 76/77, 78, 79, 81, 87, 91, 92/93, 94/95, 96, 101 (top), 102/103, 105 (both), 106, 115, 117, 121 (both); Chris Smith, pp. 127, 133; Phil Smith, p. 112 (top); South Coast Press, pp. 19, 29; Sport & General, pp. 10 (top), 54/55, 63 (top); Sporting Pictures, pp. 11, 15, 86, 101 (bottom), 124 (bottom), 125; Syndication International, p. 16; *The Times*, p. 43; Colin Turner, p. 130; Colin Wallace, p. 49; R. H. Wright, p. 90.

Contents

Foreword

BY BOB CHAMPION MBE

OLD JOCKEYS, like boxers, should never come back, but no one who has ever enjoyed the thrill of riding over fences at speed could possibly decline an invitation to join Desert Orchid at his work on the racecourse. If I knew I would be riding him next season I'd set about losing weight right now.

Desert Orchid is a jockey's dream, so much more than a quick, bold, exciting jumper whose colour makes him so attractive to the public. I was too young to appreciate Arkle but in all the time I've been involved in racing I've never known a horse with so much charisma as Desert Orchid. He is almost a freak in a nice way. He wins at all distances, on all types of going and in the same year, too. Any jockey worth the name would give his right arm to ride him.

At the races we've seen him go round time and again like a king. He clearly enjoys every minute of it, every part of the job. Walking round the paddock, cantering to the start and, of course, the race itself. He even had his ears pricked when he came prancing back after that nasty, uncharacteristic tumble at Liverpool.

I don't know why the Burridges chose David Elsworth as their trainer but it must be the best thing they have ever done.

I used to work for Toby Balding at the same time as him and a little later I was lucky enough to ride some winners for David in his early days with Colonel Vallance. What struck me about him then was that he always knew the true potential of his horses. When he said that they would win they did. He had this way of understanding them. There are times even now when you get the feeling he thinks like a horse. Certainly I don't know a trainer who thinks more about his horses. In those early days he would buy them cheaply off the flat and often improve them three stone. He is a master at training.

A lot has been said about Simon Sherwood's sympathetic riding of Desert Orchid, but he would be the first to admit that Colin Brown did all the hard work when the horse was very headstrong and much too brave for comfort. By the time Simon took over he was very nearly the finished article.

I've heard one or two people suggest Desert Orchid should be retired now. That would be madness. He was born to race and no one does it better. While he remains fit and enjoys himself I hope he will be allowed to continue to give us so much pleasure. Life would be infinitely duller without him.

The moment of a lifetime. After seven years of honest endeavour Desert Orchid wins the Gold Cup.

Simon Sherwood raises his arm in jubilation

CHAPTER ONE

'Everybody's favourite'

THE RESULT of the 1989 Tote Gold Cup at Cheltenham was as near perfection as is possible in the unpredictable world of horseracing. Snow, rain and sleet had swept across the course incessantly since dawn, at one stage putting the meeting in jeopardy. The decision was taken to carry on and the record crowd of over 50,000 already assembled had cause to be eternally grateful as a handsome grey horse named Desert Orchid, with a noble head and a heart of iron, claimed as improbable and moving a victory as has ever been witnessed on that final, pitiless hill.

The grey's adventurous, spring-heeled jumping had long before ensured his elevation to folk hero. But even gazelles cannot leap so joyously from clinging mud and there were times in the compelling later stages of the race when it seemed that slogging through the saturated ground had drained his last reserves of energy. In the end Desert Orchid's indomitable spirit helped him to rise above the awful conditions and his final victory charge touched the hearts of the nation.

Simon Sherwood, his elegant rider, his owners, James Burridge, a retired lawyer, his son, Richard, and their long-time friend, Simon Bullimore, also a lawyer, were dismayed at the unexpected deterioration in the weather. The previous day's racing had taken place in sunny, almost summer weather on good ground that would have suited Desert Orchid perfectly. But when Richard Burridge arrived at the course shortly before 10 a.m. on Thursday, snow clung to the hills around Cheltenham like an enveloping cloak and the doubts began to come crowding in. Later he was to confess, 'I hope they call it off. It just would not be fair to him.'

Simon Sherwood, too, was deeply unhappy. He had woken at a friend's home close to Cheltenham to find that 3 inches of snow had fallen. When he reached the course and realised conditions were worsening by the minute he also hoped the meeting might be abandoned so that the Gold Cup could be run on better ground a month later. But David Elsworth, the

Tension shows on the faces of Simon Sherwood, Janice Coyle and Peter Maughan as Desert Orchid is led out onto the course

Early in the race Desert Orchid is quick and accurate as ever while to his right the eventual second Yahoo jumps clumsily

Over the fence in front of the stands

trainer with an uncanny knowledge and understanding of horses, felt instinctively that Desert Orchid could win despite the worst ravages of the weather. Elsworth remained resolute and won the doubters over. Desert Orchid was already the outstanding steeplechaser in the country. He had earned his Gold Cup chance. He must run. The nation expected it.

Even so, Simon Sherwood felt unbearably pessimistic as he sloshed through the driving rain to the start, but beneath him Desert Orchid was blissfully unaware of all the last-minute anxiety. He has only one way of running and setting off as eagerly as ever landed just ahead over the first fence and raced out into the country at a sensible pace hugging the left-handed running rail. Relaxed and content, he was allowed to dictate matters to his jockey's surprise and delight.

Carvill's Hill, the hope of Ireland, fell heavily at the seventh, trapped by his inexperience, and sweeping downhill for the first time the other jockeys still unwisely allowed Desert Orchid to control the tempo of the race. Cavvies Clown, also trained by David Elsworth, came up briefly to head his stable companion after a circuit but Desert Orchid was quickly back in front. Ten Plus, a typical stamp of powerful, old-fashioned chaser, was the one who soon emerged as the most serious threat. His jockey,

11

Kevin Mooney, taking the race by the scruff of the neck, made a decisive thrust for glory and started to push clear. When Desert Orchid blundered uncharacteristically and expensively at the fourth-last fence, Ten Plus was suddenly holding a useful advantage. 'That mistake stopped him quite badly for a moment,' Simon Sherwood admitted later.

The notorious third-last fence at the foot of a sharp downhill run has more than once decided the outcome of the Gold Cup and now it was to do so again. Ten Plus was still just in front, galloping relentlessly, when he failed to jump quite high enough, clipped the top and collapsed on landing thus leaving Desert Orchid once more in the lead.

The cheers that rang out to greet the muddy grey were premature and quickly dimmed as the unconsidered outsider Yahoo swept past on the inside, moving with ominous ease for the legions of racegoers beseeching Desert Orchid to win. Soon, Yahoo was two lengths clear of the grey, who drifted right-handed on the final bend as so often before, giving away precious yards. Peter O'Sullevan, the voice of racing, echoed the fears of millions of viewers on BBC television as he commented, 'Desert Orchid looks as though he's tiring in the ground.'

But now, with grim, stubborn determination, Desert Orchid was fighting back more bravely than he had ever done before. Slowly, gradually, inexorably, advancing stride by stride, he was clawing his way back and though he conceded another vital half length at the last fence by cleverly shuffling his step to make sure of a clean jump, the task no longer seemed impossible. For the first time in their matchless unbeaten partnership that already stretched to eight victories, Simon Sherwood was being really serious with Desert Orchid. Three, four, five times his whip fell on the horse's almost white quarters.

The response was even more than any of us could have wished or dreamed. The questions were more about character and raw courage than ability and thrillingly, unbelievably, a hundred yards after the final fence Desert Orchid was once more back in front. As he completed his glorious victory charge he dived sharply left-handed, of all things, as if to intimidate poor Yahoo on the far rail. Sherwood confirmed, 'It was his way of telling Yahoo to shove off, and elbow him out of it.'

Desert Orchid darted left so aggressively that Sherwood was forced to stop riding for an instant, put down his whip in his right hand and haul him off his opponent, who had been in danger of being barged onto the rails. There could be only one winner now and as Desert Orchid strode clear, roared on by 50,000 pleading voices, the crescendo of acclamation set off wave after wave of highly charged emotion around the racecourse.

Ten Plus (No 11) who was to die tragically a few minutes later, chases Desert Orchid over another fence

The last fence amd Yahoo is still just ahead as Desert Orchid prepares for his compelling late victory charge on the steep uphill finish

Moments after the last jump both jockeys gather and balance their horses for the final battle

A wonderful close-up of horse and jockey working in unison as they drive for the line

Those of us lucky enough to be there knew we had witnessed one of the supreme moments of sport.

Tom Morgan, who had ridden such an enterprising race on Yahoo, trotted over and patted the grey's neck with wonder in his eyes. Simon Sherwood seemed overcome as he gently and gratefully tweaked his partner's pricked ears.

The race had been so tough in the ghastly conditions that only five finished from the thirteen who had set out. Mud covered Desert Orchid's legs up to his flanks as he began a hero's return through the massive, cheering crowd. Richard Burridge was the first to reach him, immediately followed by the horse's elfin-faced lass, Janice Coyle, and travelling head lad, Peter

A victory salute from Simon Sherwood as Desert Orchid returns in the rain to a tumultuous welcome

Maughan. Progress was understandably slow as they fought their way through lines of people anxious to see and reach out and touch the grey marvel who had lightened all our lives. Sherwood's hand was shaken twenty times by complete strangers. So they made their way back through a rising tide of emotion to the hallowed winner's enclosure amid unforgettable scenes of jubilation. Hundreds of racegoers invaded the area.

As the television cameras faithfully followed Cheltenham's finest grey celebrity on his victory march, Peter O'Sullevan told his viewers, 'Desert Orchid. The 5–2 favourite. Everybody's favourite. . . .'

Three cheers were called for Desert Orchid and rousingly

Desert Orchid is surrounded by jubilant supporters as he makes his way back through the paddock to a wildly emotional reception in the winner's enclosure

given. The calmest individual on the course seemed to be the grey wonder at the centre of all the attention and adulation. Ears pricked, he looked around him with that bright, almost quizzical way of his, surely aware of what he had achieved. Colin Brown, for so long Desert Orchid's jockey, rushed to greet his old comrade and hugged Janice Coyle. While Mrs Midge Burridge embraced Desert Orchid a burly punter rushed up and planted a kiss firmly on Simon Sherwood's cheek. When the instruction was given for the horses to be led away some of the crowd voiced their displeasure because they wished to admire Desert Orchid for a little longer. How they cheered again when he was given an unscheduled lap of honour.

In a televised interview with me immediately afterwards Simon Sherwood could scarcely hold back the tears.

'I've never known a horse as brave. He hated the conditions and dug as deep as he could possibly go. Two or three times I thought I was beaten, but he kept finding a little bit more. He's quite amazing. The best by a long, long way,' he added, to further applause from the crowd who had gathered around us.

'Haven't we met before,' the grey seems to be saying to jump racing's most popular patron as Richard and James Burridge look on with unmistakable pride

James Burridge, the man who had bred Desert Orchid, stepped proudly up to receive the Gold Cup from the Queen Mother, followed by David Elsworth and Simon Sherwood. Richard Burridge was so overcome that he threatened to give the first silent interview when he spoke on television.

'I can hardly describe how I feel, just completely overwhelmed,' he croaked. 'My glasses had misted up and I could not see much from the lawn after the last but I knew he was going to get Yahoo by the crowd's reaction. He is all heart and just won't give in. How I shall treasure this day. I know I will never experience anything like this feeling again. It was hard work fighting back along the passage with him afterwards. I felt as if I had done three and a quarter miles.'

Later the Burridges and their fellow owner, Simon Bullimore, were invited to the Royal box for a much longer chat with the Queen Mother.

Desert Orchid's stirring victory in the Gold Cup was his twenty-seventh success in seven years of honest endeavour and took his earnings surging past £400,000, easily a record for a

Richard Burridge gives Desert Orchid a grateful pat as Janice Coyle gazes adoringly at everyone's favourite grey

After the official business of a dope test former jockey Paul Elliott helps Janice give Desert Orchid a quick bath

jumper. David Elsworth, the trainer whose rock-solid resolve to run had made it all possible, reflected quietly, 'This is a very special moment. I am so very, very proud of this horse.'

Many miles away in Newmarket, Lester Piggott, who years earlier had ridden Desert Orchid's sire, Grey Mirage, to several victories, watched the race on television and then delivered his verdict with unashamed admiration: 'That Desert Orchid is just like a human being. He knows exactly what he is doing in a race. He is a star,' he said. No one could possibly wish to disagree.

Horse racing is sometimes dismissed as an irrelevance, but not on Thursday, 16 March 1989. The splendour of Desert Orchid's achievements warranted photographs on the front pages of five daily newspapers the next morning. But the fuller reports on the inside echoed the bleakness at the death of Ten Plus, who had broken a leg in his fall and later had to be destroyed.

Ten Plus died doing what he enjoyed best. He was bred to run and jump and years of patient handling by the grand old master of training, Fulke Walwyn, had at last seen him emerge as the complete article, tough, brave, resolute and full of class. Ten Plus possessed an endearing enthusiasm for the game he embellished and his death was a grim reminder of the price horses sometimes pay for our entertainment. Triumph and tragedy stood shoulder to shoulder that extraordinary afternoon at Cheltenham and the awareness that jump racing can be unbearably cruel at times merely heightened the universal pleasure at Desert Orchid's achievement.

There is no doubt who is the most important person at Whitsbury the morning after the Gold Cup

CHAPTER TWO

Early days

DESERT ORCHID's family background offers few if any clues of the brilliance to come. In the very best tradition of luck and coincidence, which has certainly improved with the telling, James Burridge found Desert Orchid's granddam Grey Orchid in a remote field near Newark. She had won a point-to-point as a five-year-old but was then, according to Burridge, abandoned to a life of solitude at grass.

Burridge was looking for a suitable hunter and became interested when he realised that Grey Orchid had escaped from the field, where he had been sent to inspect her, into an adjoining one across an imposing hedge. The mare looked woolly, muddy and cold and Burridge says, improbably, that icicles were hanging from her. But he liked her colour and she became his property for £175. Grey Orchid proved to be by the stallion No Orchid out of an obscure mare, Harbour Lights, who in turn was by the sprinter, Portlaw.

James Burridge took her home, cleaned her up, led her out into the stable yard, climbed onto a mounting block, eased himself into the saddle and found himself somersaulting backwards onto a manure heap under the mare. Fate can play strange tricks, as Burridge points out with chilling clarity.

'If the manure heap had not been there, she would have broken her back and I would have been dead!'

Next time he wisely mounted her in a nearby field. The result was again explosive and almost as dangerous. Grey Orchid charged round the field, throwing her head back repeatedly into her rider's face. Burridge persisted with the mare. They shared a common bond of stubbornness. Spirited rather than wilful, she offered a rare challenge to her new owner in the hunting field and eventually, to his eternal credit, he won a point-to-point on her. It was a triumph of persistence.

When James Burridge decided to breed from Grey Orchid he put her first to an anonymous stallion, Blackness, but the resulting foal died of a twisted gut. Next he sent her to be mated with a Hunters' Improvement Society stallion named Brother. Burridge recalls: 'Grey Orchid was wild but she had the right

Flower Child, dam of Desert Orchid, was acclaimed as National Hunt broodmare of 1988. James Burridge (right), the man whose foresight made this story possible, receives his award from the Agriculture Minister John MacGregor

spirit, just like Desert Orchid years later. Brother cost me £20 and the result was Desert Orchid's mother, Flower Child.' So much for the detailed planning of mating arrangements at the more sophisticated studs. Brother was chosen chiefly because he was local, available and inexpensive.

Flower Child, too, proved hopelessly headstrong in the hunting field. James Burridge, now a retired company lawyer, was then an enthusiastic follower to hounds. He was close to 14 stone but weight did not seem to bother Flower Child as she outjumped some of the best hunters in the county. The mare relished dashing across country but her natural impatience made her an awkward, uncomfortable ride during the lengthy stops and pauses that are all part of a day's hunting. Eventually James Burridge acknowledged, with some relief, that he no longer enjoyed the prospect of hunting on Flower Child.

'I'd pray for the meet to be off for any reason,' he once told me.

So, at the rather late age of eight, Flower Child was given a fresh challenge in point-to-points. All the familiar family traits were evident in her manner of racing even though she was pulled up four times in succession. She was a brave if somewhat impetuous jumper, always tried to lead and invariably tired long before the end of her races. Even so, she showed her owner sufficient promise to justify sending her into training with Charlie James, near Lambourn in Berkshire. Most mares of that age would already have had foals at stud. Who knows what quirk of fate persuaded Burridge to pursue such an unorthodox course with Flower Child?

James remembers: 'At first she was a complete tearaway and when we tried to school her over fences she wanted to jump the post and rails surrounding the schooling field. She was not that good but the one thing that turned her on was her jumping. She was the bravest mare ever, a great trier.'

In three busy seasons Flower Child managed to win two minor chases and in one of them she was the sole finisher. The only time she ever fell was at the huge, gaping Chair fence at Aintree in the Topham Trophy. Flower Child's form was perhaps modest but she was consistent, her limbs were sound, she was undeniably competitive and she relished jumping. You could not ask for better ingredients for a broodmare and so at the extremely late age of eleven Flower Child was retired to the paddocks in 1978.

James Burridge chose for her first covering, at a cost of £350, Grey Mirage, a top-class colt on the flat as a three-year-old in 1972 when he started third favourite in the 2,000 Guineas and finished unplaced ridden by Lester Piggott. Grey Mirage was trained, by a curious coincidence, at Whitsbury by Bill Marshall. Grey Mirage failed to win at distances longer than seven furlongs. Speed was his finest quality and he was syndicated at £2,000 a share to stand at the Ticklerton Stud in Shropshire. He was to prove neither fashionable nor particularly successful as a sire of flat horses and so, like countless good honest horses before and since, was exported abroad, to Saudi Arabia, where he later died.

Desert Orchid, his finest son, was born in 1979. He proved a lively foal at the Burridge estate, near Melton Mowbray, bigger and stronger than his mother, Flower Child, who died in 1988. In January 1989, shortly after her death, she was named by the Thoroughbred Breeders' Association as National Hunt Brood-mare of the Year and James Burridge travelled to London to collect his award at their annual lunch. When Desert Orchid

was a yearling James Burridge's son came to see him. Richard shared his father's love of racing and once spent time working as a boardman in a betting shop.

He recalls: 'Really the yearling was not very impressive at all. At first I thought he was scraggy and scrawny and completely unco-ordinated.'

Once more fate took a powerful hand. As the two Burridges, father and son, inspected the raw-boned young grey, he took off across the field, galloping flat out. Now, instantly, Richard Burridge was deeply interested.

'Suddenly a bell went off in the back of my head. He was the most wonderful mover and anything seemed possible. I decided to negotiate there and then to buy a controlling interest in him.' When the deal was concluded Richard Burridge owned 50 per cent of Desert Orchid, his father retained 25 per cent and the final quarter share was taken by a family friend, Simon Bullimore.

Desert Orchid is a most popular attraction at local shows in Leicestershire

Once, as a skittish young horse, Desert Orchid escaped from his paddock and galloped loose on a busy main road for twenty-five minutes before he was caught. This time fortune favoured the brave and the horse was in a much calmer condition than his anguished captors when they returned home. Later, at three, when he was broken in, he showed much of the strong-willed character of his mother and grandmother. Like them he was not so much wayward, simply high spirited.

In 1982 the decision was taken to put Desert Orchid in training with David Elsworth, a gifted young trainer already offering promise of the brilliant years ahead. Elsworth has an affinity with horses that is matched by few if any of his competitors. Genius is a word used much too liberally today but it is a description that fits him comfortably. For years he had been a heavy, capable and not very successful jump jockey but the experience of working for a variety of trainers had been put to

David Elsworth's instinctive understanding of Desert Orchid was to prove vital in the years ahead

good use and it was Elsworth, then assistant to Colonel Ricky Vallance, who orchestrated the triumph of the stable's Red Candle in the Mackeson Gold Cup and, a year later, over Red Rum in the Hennessy Gold Cup. But when Vallance lost his licence Elsworth was out of a job and unable to work in racing.

It was a bitter reverse for David and Jane Elsworth, who had a young family to support. A man of not inconsiderable resource, Elsworth spent some time as a stallholder at country markets in Wiltshire and Dorset, selling fabric and cloth wherever he could find a regular pitch. But racing pulled him back as irresistibly as a magnet. In 1977 he started a livery business on the edge of Salisbury Plain in a cattle yard in the tiny village of Figheldean. The following June, encouraged by his wife, he applied for his own licence and by September he was at last a trainer with a handful of equine oddities and miles of Army tank ranges for gallops.

He remembers: 'Oh yes, it was a terrible struggle for a while but once we had horses around us again it was always fun. I never did find racing difficult. It's just like cards. With the right hand you collect the pot. But you can't win if you don't play . . . and I was out of the game for far too long.'

Instantly successful, he soon moved to larger stables, first at Lucknam Park, near Chippenham, then to the superbly equipped Whitsbury estate on the Hampshire Downs, near Fordingbridge. Here Sir Gordon Richards and later Bill Marshall had trained with success. You could not find better gallops in the country, though Elsworth once assured me quite seriously that you could train a horse on a tennis court if it was good enough. Richard Burridge liked what he'd heard about David Elsworth, who was proving equally adept at winning races on the flat and over jumps. Burridge also felt it was important that he trained in isolation away from the major horseracing centres. Whatever the reason Elsworth proved an inspired choice.

Horses arrive and depart constantly at a busy and successful mixed training stable like Whitsbury. Desert Orchid, still rather plain, almost iron grey in colour and distinctly immature, made an immediate impact on his new trainer for the very good reason that he would not come out of the horsebox that had brought him on the long journey from Leicestershire. No amount of coaxing could persuade him to change his mind so Elsworth turned him round and helped him backwards down the ramp. Once more Desert Orchid showed the intractable character that was to be his hallmark in future years. He steadfastly refused to enter the stable allotted to him. Again the trainer turned him round and eased him through the door without further complaint.

CHAPTER THREE

'An absolute natural'

EVERYONE LOVES A GREY and Gary Morgan, a young apprentice who weighed barely 7 stone, was delighted to be given the chance to look after Desert Orchid. The new inmate at Whitsbury soon learned to enter and leave his box in the conventional manner and showed a pleasing willingness in his attitude to his daily work. But he was, at times, much too keen.

'He had no patience,' recalls Morgan. 'Just wanted to tear off, and he was always strong from the start.'

Quite simply Desert Orchid loved to run. Given half a chance he would rush headlong up the gallops, testing the strength and nerve of his riders. Many young horses are keen and pull hard at home when they first come into training. So often they become jaded, cunning or plain disinterested along the way. What is unusual about Desert Orchid is that in his eleventh year he still retains the same boyish enthusiasm for the morning's task and even now there are times when it seems that Rodney Boult, his hugely experienced work rider, is barely in control. Boult, a spry, neat little man, his face weathered by ten thousand mornings on the downs, once regularly rode the Derby winner Shirley Heights in his days with John Dunlop. Old-fashioned, disciplined, skilful, hard-working stablemen who care more about their horses than themselves are priceless in these days of shifting labour in racing and David Elsworth was delighted to bring Rodney Boult to Whitsbury as his head lad.

Colin Brown, a busy, bustling jockey, honest and reliable, was riding most of Elsworth's horses at the time. He remembers Desert Orchid in those early days as a free-running type, not very big but with an unusually powerful neck. It was Brown who first schooled the grey over a set of four practice hurdles and that unexpectedly joyful experience set the seal on a partnership that was to reach the very top in racing in the years ahead.

'He just took off outside the wings and was from one side to the other in a moment. An absolute natural,' says the jockey.

A novices' hurdle at Kempton was chosen for Desert Orchid's

Firm friends and regular partners on the gallops each morning. Desert Orchid and head lad Rodney Boult

introduction to racing in January 1983. Since he was both weak and backward, and several of the runners were experienced handicappers from the flat, he was sent to Kempton without any heady expectations. Desert Orchid drifted out to 50–1 for his first race, the Walton Novices' Hurdle, and there was not a hint of the drama to come as he rushed down to the start, his head held high. Colin Brown had quite a task trying to restrain him in the middle of the field but was just succeeding when a horse fell directly in front of them, pitching his jockey Robert Stronge perilously onto the ground.

Desert Orchid, already jumping with the boldness that was

to become his trademark, took off outside the wings of that hurdle and landed with a sickening thud on Robert Stronge's head. Poor Colin Brown feared the worst but Desert Orchid was unaware of what had happened and turned into the straight making ground on the leaders.

Lack of fitness then began to tell and he was a very tired horse as he approached the final hurdle. What happened next is etched firmly in the memory of everyone who was at Kempton that day. Desert Orchid met the hurdle wrong, tried to make one final valiant, exuberant leap, crashed through the timber, fell heavily and lay as if unconscious as the remaining runners scrambled past.

Colin Brown, believing the horse was merely winded, quickly loosened his girths and removed the saddle but to those of us in the stands, including the Burridges, who hurried down the course to the last flight, it seemed far more serious.

After several minutes the racecourse vet and his anxious helpers, including Gary Morgan, rolled the stricken horse over without any obvious sign of improvement in his condition. After a further lengthy pause James Burridge was warned that screens might have to be erected around Desert Orchid if he had been seriously injured. For one ghastly moment it seemed like the end. Then suddenly and wonderfully the horse shook his head and scrambled to his feet to cheers from the stands.

James Burridge has never forgotten that bleak scene and believes Desert Orchid was down for fully twelve minutes. He recalls: 'The vet, who was very efficient, felt he might be badly hurt. Luckily he was just exhausted after winding himself but it was the most horrible experience. When he did get to his feet I remember thinking I would never race him again. But he's so tough and enthusiastic he was fine the next day.'

As the relieved group walked back with Desert Orchid, David Elsworth's comment to James Burridge vividly illustrated the trainer's extraordinary insight into the character of the horse he had known for only a few weeks.

Elsworth insisted: 'The problem with most horses is to get 95 per cent of their potential from them. The trouble with this one is stopping him from giving you 105 per cent.'

The trainer considered taking Desert Orchid to a racecourse two or three times without running him to help his recovery from such an unpleasant experience. But the grey seemed the least concerned by what had happened. He went home, ate his supper without a moment's hesitation and was his usual bouncy self the next morning.

'You would not know he'd had a race. It just didn't bother him,' says Gary Morgan, the surprise still in his voice.

A day at the seaside for Colin Brown and the nation's favourite grey

Robert Stronge, too, emerged unscathed, much to Colin Brown's relief when he returned to the jockeys' changing room at Kempton. Stronge's helmet had taken the full impact of Desert Orchid's hooves and he did not even have a headache!

Desert Orchid's run a month later at Wincanton confirmed that there were no lasting effects from his fall. He jumped well enough but again tired in the closing stages and finished in the

ruck. It was a satisfactory performance in the circumstances. Just over a fortnight later came the first glimpse of his true potential. Desert Orchid was taking on older horses for the first time but was backed at odds of 7–1 in an open race. He settled better early on, made progress turning into the straight, jumped the last flight like an old handicapper and finished to such purpose that he would have caught the winner, Diamond Hunter, in a few more strides. The fact that Diamond Hunter just held on by a neck in a photo finish proved to be the most enormous bonus for Desert Orchid because he was able to start the following season as a maiden. Had he prevailed at Sandown his second season as a hurdler would have been infinitely harder.

He ran once more, finishing unplaced in unsuitably heavy ground at Newbury, and returned home for a long summer's rest at grass. When he came back into training at Whitsbury the following autumn the change in his physical condition was unmistakable. A new star was about to emerge.

*The fall at Kempton that so nearly
ended Desert Orchid's career in his
first race. He lay winded for fully
twelve minutes at the last hurdle
before scrambling to his feet to the
intense relief of everyone present*

CHAPTER FOUR

A season to remember

Gary Morgan leads out Desert Orchid for his last race of the season at Sandown. Note how very much darker he was as a young horse

GARY MORGAN'S DREAMS extended beyond leading up winners. He wanted to ride them, too. A neat apprentice jockey, he failed by only a short head to win on the 20–1 chance Julesian, trained by David Elsworth, in a race on the flat at Bath in the summer of 1983. Gary was ambitious but opportunities were restricted. He stayed at Whitsbury a little longer then moved elsewhere on the promise of more rides but it was not until the spring of 1989 that he finally achieved that elusive first victory as a jockey on Tremmin at Ludlow.

He has followed Desert Orchid's career with delight but not surprise. 'He was a nice horse to look after and I always thought he'd turn out all right. You can always tell a good horse but at the time I did not realise he was going to be that good,' he says. When Gary Morgan departed from Whitsbury his place as Desert Orchid's groom was taken by Jackie Parrish, a girl who had worked for Elsworth from the moment he came to Whitsbury.

The grey was so much stronger at the start of the 1983–4 season that it was decided to adopt new tactics. Until then Colin Brown had fought manfully, trying to teach him to relax in the hope that it would help him conserve some of his energy for the finish. Now trainer and jockey agreed it might be easier to give the horse his head and let him bowl along in front. Desert Orchid's free-running, bold-jumping style of racing proved an instant success in a novices' hurdle at Ascot on firm ground on 29 October 1983. Starting second favourite at 11–8, he set off gaily in front, was soon well clear and though tiring a little towards the end won unchallenged by twenty lengths from Lucky Rascal. It was a pattern that would be gloriously and frequently repeated over the next six years.

Desert Orchid won again, this time at odds-on, on his next visit to Ascot three weeks later. Those first victories had been over two miles on firm ground. Now David Elsworth felt he was ready to tackle longer distances and so he returned to Sandown for the December Novices' Hurdle over two miles,

five furlongs and seventy-five yards. Once more the ground was firm and once more Desert Orchid was an odds-on favourite but the final seventy-five yards proved just beyond him. He led, as usual, soaring thrillingly over his hurdles, sometimes gaining lengths in the air, and was still in front at the last flight, but Catch Phrase had already proved his stamina by winning over three miles and he collared Desert Orchid on the climb to the post. The winning margin was only three-quarters of a length. Time was to prove that extreme distance would not trouble Desert Orchid, especially at Sandown, but on that day he was just outstayed by a very useful hurdler who, significantly, was a year older.

Next Desert Orchid returned to Kempton, scene of that ghastly fall at the start of his career. By now he was a mature racing machine, fully ready for the test posed by the opposition in the Foodbrokers Armour Novices' Hurdle on 26 December. This was the first time he was not ridden in a race by Colin Brown. Boxing Day is one of those frustrating racing days when leading jockeys are torn between promising rides at several

Ascot, 29 October 1983, and the first win of Desert Orchid who was to become the most popular racehorse since Arkle

Jackie Parrish, the stable girl who took over the care of Desert Orchid when Gary Morgan left Whitsbury

meetings. David Elsworth was sending the useful mare Buckbe to Wincanton and Colin Brown also had the chance of another good mount there, King's Bishop. So he took the road to Wincanton and duly landed a double on Buckbe and King's Bishop. His decision was helped by the knowledge that Richard Burridge had promised he would continue to partner Desert Orchid in the future.

Richard Linley was the lucky young rider who was chosen as substitute for Colin Brown on Desert Orchid at Kempton. The change of jockey certainly did not affect the horse. Once again he made all the running and won unchallenged.

Richard Linley, an intelligent, articulate man who is now an Inspector of Courses for the Jockey Club, kept the video of that race and still watches it occasionally.

He recalls, 'Desert Orchid was a bit bright and breezy. We were twenty lengths clear by the second hurdle. Going off in front was the only choice you had. He did not leave you any alternative.'

Colin Brown was back in the saddle when Desert Orchid

TOP: *Desert Orchid is, for once, not fluent at the final hurdle against Catch Phrase at Sandown*

ABOVE: *An easy success for Desert Orchid and Colin Brown in the Tolworth Hurdle at Sandown on 7 January 1984*

LEFT: *A new jockey, Richard Linley, but the same result. Desert Orchid runs right away from the opposition at Kempton on Boxing Day, 1983*

Desert Orchid's springheeled jumping takes him clear of top class opposition in the Kingwell Pattern Hurdle at Wincanton on 23 February 1984. Now for the Champion Hurdle

continued his season of excellence at Sandown a fortnight later in the Tolworth Hurdle. The outstanding champion jockey John Francome, who had twice finished second to the grey previously, was on I Haventalight this time and was determined to prevent Desert Orchid poaching his customary lead. Francome and I Haventalight pressed and harried him for a few seconds on the inside but soon, inevitably, irresistibly, the grey ran away from his rivals and there he stayed, to Francome's evident frustration.

After another facile victory at Ascot the decision was taken to pitch Desert Orchid against some of the best hurdlers in training in the Kingwell Pattern Hurdle at Wincanton, long established as a serious trial for the Waterford Crystal Champion Hurdle at the Cheltenham Festival the following month. Desert Orchid was still a novice and the going was softer than he had encountered all season but the others were the ones who appeared inconvenienced as he stormed round the tight Somerset track in total control. Stan's Pride, a tough and resolute mare trained on the Welsh borders, tried to challenge on the downhill run to the final flight but Desert Orchid shook her off with accustomed ease and raced home first by four lengths, with Very Promising a further twelve lengths back. It was a stunning display of exuberant running and jumping by the grey, who was now being taken very seriously indeed by the bookmakers compiling ante-post odds for the major races at Cheltenham. David Elsworth had backed Desert Orchid each way for the Champion at 66–1 early in February. After Wincanton his odds tumbled to 14–1 and by the day of the race his price was down to 7–1 second favourite.

'We respect the favourite Dawn Run but we're not frightened

of anyone,' the trainer told newsmen. 'Sometimes in life you're lucky to come across something very special like Desert Orchid.'

The total eclipse of Desert Orchid in the 1984 Champion Hurdle was the first of five consecutive defeats at the annual Cheltenham Festival. Elsworth's hopes and Brown's plans were in tatters soon after halfway. Dawn Run, a big, imposing, aggressive racemare took the battle to Desert Orchid from the very start and Colin Brown found, to his dismay, that he was struggling to stay with her. He confirms: 'I thought Desert Orchid was already a very good horse and I could not believe how easily Dawn Run was going just in front of us jumping the second hurdle. She was absolutely cruising and we were already struggling.'

Desert Orchid showed his character by briefly forcing his way into the lead but it was no more than a gesture. Dawn Run swept past him again soon after half way and he quickly dropped

A rare defeat for Desert Orchid in a season of excellence. He is already beaten as the imposing mare Dawn Run heads for a famous victory in the Waterford Crystal Champion Hurdle

out of contention. Perhaps he was a year too young for such a severe test. Certainly he tended to drift right-handed, giving away some ground. As his owners and trainer digested Colin Brown's disconsolate report after the race, a few yards away Mrs Charmian Hill, the eccentric owner of the victorious Dawn Run, was being tossed high in the air by jubilant supporters.

It was a disappointing conclusion to a memorable season for Desert Orchid. He had won six times before the unexpected reverse at Cheltenham. Some trainers might have been tempted to put him straight over fences the following season. David Elsworth, however, felt he deserved one more year as a hurdler.

When Desert Orchid returned into training at the start of his second season in the autumn of 1983, his younger half-brother Ragged Robin, by Baragoi out of Flower Child, was sent to Whitsbury with him. Ragged Robin, a dark bay gelding, was only three when he finished third in his first race over hurdles and was later placed once more from four outings. It was a satisfactory enough first season, which offered promise for the future.

Just like his illustrious half-brother, he made significant improvement the following year, winning three times and finishing third in a valuable hurdle at Chepstow. He was proving to be a tough, consistent competitor and although quite small already looked every inch a most exciting prospect as a chaser. Certainly David Elsworth thought so. But after the summer's break Ragged Robin did not accompany Desert Orchid back to Whitsbury. He was sent instead to begin his chasing career with another trainer, Tim Forster, at Letcombe Bassett, near Wantage. Forster is one of the finest jump trainers of his generation, a man who much prefers chasers to hurdlers, and he has won the Grand National three times.

In normal circumstances you could not possibly choose a better man to train a young horse over fences but when you consider Desert Orchid's meteoric career, the decision by James and John Burridge to move Ragged Robin seems inexplicable. Perhaps they felt David Elsworth did not have sufficient experience with steeplechasers. Whatever the reason, David Elsworth was deeply hurt when he was told Ragged Robin would be going elsewhere.

The contentious transfer of Ragged Robin briefly put a serious strain on the relationship between Desert Orchid's owners and trainer. But the common bond they shared in their love and belief in him helped heal the wounds. Much, much later James Burridge assured me he had not realised for one moment just how offended David Elsworth would be at the departure of Ragged Robin to Letcombe Bassett.

Desert Orchid's talented half brother, the ill-fated Ragged Robin, whose switch to another trainer briefly put a strain on the relationship between David Elsworth and the Burridges

Ragged Robin continued his winning ways with Tim Forster, first in a warm-up race over hurdles, then on his debut over fences at Hereford in a race that fully illustrated the hazards of jump racing. Three horses came down at the very first fence. By the time Ragged Robin and his jockey Richard Dunwoody stumbled through the wreckage they were well behind. They recovered to such effect that they were closing on the leader, Welsh Oak, when he fell at the final fence. Ragged Robin won comfortably in the end but it was to be his last victory. Regrettably his jumping was becoming increasingly suspect. He fell at Sandown, unseated his jockey in his next race then broke a leg when he fell again at Worcester. The racecourse vet took the only realistic option, which was to put him down to avoid unnecessary suffering.

Ragged Robin, so far, is the only produce of Flower Child to win other than Desert Orchid. In 1987 James Burridge put another half-sister, by Workboy, into training with David Elsworth as a two-year-old. Named Peacework, she ran with considerable promise in her first race, finishing fifth over seven furlongs at Goodwood, but was then rather disappointing. Tried over hurdles in the winter of 1988–9, she proved hard-headed and impossibly headstrong in three races and so in an attempt to calm her down she was sent to Sussex to be covered by the stallion Pitpan before resuming her career on the flat with another trainer, Colin Bravery. James Burridge also has two young half-sisters to Desert Orchid at his home, the 14-acre Ab Kettleby Stud near Melton Mowbray.

CHAPTER FIVE

Blinkers!

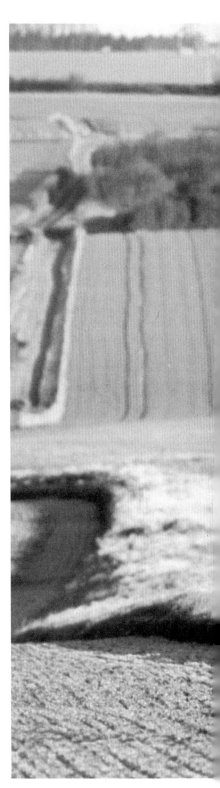

D ESERT ORCHID found the going much tougher in 1984–5. This often happens to horses who have swept the board the previous season. Then his improvement as a novice had been nothing short of remarkable. Now he was being asked to take on the best hurdlers, often on disadvantageous terms. Though he was frequently beaten and once, surprisingly, equipped with blinkers, a piece of equipment usually tried on ungenuine horses, no one could possibly doubt his courage or commitment.

He began with a satisfactory run into third place behind Ra Nova in the Captain Quist Hurdle at Kempton and was again third at Ascot, seven lengths behind See You Then. Since See You Then ended the season by winning the Champion Hurdle and the pair had met at level weights at Ascot, Desert Orchid's performance could scarcely be described as disappointing. At Kempton on Boxing Day he reversed the form with See You Then but was unable to cope with the mercurial Browne's Gazette, who sprinted fifteen lengths clear on the run-in.

Jackie Parrish now accompanied Desert Orchid on his first trip abroad to Ireland for the Irish Sweeps Hurdle at Leopardstown on 12 January. They made the long and tiring journey by boat in heavy seas and neither the horse nor his attendants were feeling in top form by the time they reached Leopardstown. Desert Orchid's task was formidable. Set to carry top weight of 12 stone, he was asked to concede as much as 2 stone to some of his rivals on a left-handed track, which Elsworth was beginning to suspect might not suit him. The grey, willing as ever, raced away in front but by the final turn the Irish jockeys were queuing up on his heels and when he jumped sharply right-handed at the second-last hurdle they poured past like dervishes on the inside. Colin Brown quickly and wisely accepted defeat and allowed Desert Orchid to coast home. He knew there would

Something to brighten the morning

be other, better days. One of them came next time at Sandown in the Oteley Hurdle on 2 February. The ground was extremely testing and once again Desert Orchid was giving weight away to good horses, but he pulled his way immediately to the front and won handsomely, by ten lengths, from Mr Moonraker.

So to Cheltenham for a second crack at the Champion Hurdle though this time he was dismissed in the betting as a 20–1 outsider. Browne's Gazette was a red-hot favourite for this race at 6–4 on but was facing the wrong way when the tapes rose

Back to form. Previous disappointments are forgotten as Desert Orchid returns to his imperious best against Mr Moonraker in the Oteley Hurdle at Sandown in February 1985

and was to be seen heading at ninety degrees away from the rest of the field. In many races that bad luck might have been overcome. But this was the Champion Hurdle, the ground was fast and two runners, Northern Trial and Desert Orchid, set off as if chased by a marauding bunch of football hooligans.

Those of us accustomed to seeing the flying grey dictate race after race could scarcely believe our eyes as Northern Trial led him by fully five or six lengths up the hill. But they were both going too fast for their own good. Desert Orchid was exhausted

by the time Colin Brown pulled him up on the approach to the second-last hurdle and Northern Trial was already out of contention when falling heavily at the final flight.

Says Colin, 'I don't know whether he was not quite right or if he sulked or what was wrong. But he was never, ever going with his usual freedom.'

That dismal display by Desert Orchid led to drastic changes for his next race, the Welsh Champion Hurdle at Chepstow on Easter Monday where he ran, at Richard Burridge's request, in blinkers. Normally blinkers, hoods and visors are used on horses who, for whatever reason, do not seem to be trying in their races. Fitting blinkers narrows their vision at the side, helps them concentrate and sometimes but not always renews their interest and enthusiasm for racing. It is unthinkable now to believe that anyone could possibly question Desert Orchid's attitude, but

RIGHT, CENTRE, BOTTOM: *The wrong way. Desert Orchid stands off too far away from the final hurdle, crashes through the top bar and falls heavily*

OPPOSITE TOP LEFT: *What a team! Desert Orchid and Jackie Parrish together in the winner's enclosure at Sandown*

OPPOSITE: *The right way. Desert Orchid skips nimbly over a hurdle on the first circuit in the Trillium Handicap Hurdle at Ascot on 13 April 1985*

blinkers were fitted over his head in the paddock and the result suggests that the horse, for one, did not appreciate the experiment. Significantly, he was never asked to wear them again. The going was impossibly heavy, even for Chepstow, and though Desert Orchid had taken his customary lead at the start he was caught and passed by four horses early in the straight. Since the cause was hopeless, Colin Brown pulled him up.

What a difference five days can make. Desert Orchid was pressed into action again the following Saturday at Ascot in the Trillium Handicap Hurdle. The going this time was good and though he carried 12 stone and was giving away lumps of weight to all his rivals there is little doubt he would have won but for a shocking fall at the final flight. Off he went in front and by the time he was approaching the last hurdle only Comedy Fair remained in attendance. Desert Orchid took off optimistically far from the hurdle but his extravagant leap was not quite enough and he crashed through the top bar on the way down, turning a violent and horrifying somersault. It was the sort of fall that can break a horse's neck and few if any of the crowd made their way to greet the winner, Comedy Fair, until they had seen Desert Orchid rise safely but somewhat shakily to his feet.

That excellent run, his best of the season, quelled any lingering doubts held by those who had previously questioned Desert Orchid's ability and enthusiasm. The time had now been reached for the next stage of his eventful career. Late that spring he was schooled over fences at Whitsbury by Colin Brown.

Colin laughs at the memory: 'It took about thirty seconds. He simply flew over them. I think David closed his eyes.'

By now Colin Brown was a publican as well as a jockey. Industrious, ambitious and astute, he had bought a free house, the Furze Bush, just outside Newbury in 1983, exactly ten years after riding his first winner. Together with his partner, his brother-in-law Tom Marshall, he developed and expanded the pub, adding a larger bar and a restaurant. Business was brisk but riding was still his first priority and only on days when he was not racing would you find him working behind the bar.

Desert Orchid remained in training a little longer than usual that season in preparation for his only flat race, the Group 3 Mono Sagaro Stakes over 2 miles at Ascot on 1 May. Ridden by Brian Rouse he pulled his way into the lead with his customary vigour and may well have wondered at the endlessly long run to the first jump. Desert Orchid stayed in front for $1\frac{1}{2}$ miles, was still fourth moving into the straight but then faded.

David Elsworth had been toying with the idea of trying to win a maiden race with him in the North. Now he concluded, 'He's much too good for flat racing.'

'Too brave for his own good'

A triumphant return after a winning debut over fences at Devon and Exeter in November 1985

DESERT ORCHID was extremely quick and fluent when schooled over fences at Whitsbury once more in the autumn of 1985, but before starting a new venture as a steeplechaser he was sent to Kempton for what seemed the simplest of tasks in the Captain Quist Hurdle. The going was fast, the opposition modest and there were plenty of punters prepared to support him even at the prohibitive odds of 9–4 on.

Colin Brown recalls: 'We were thirty lengths clear and the silly old fool turned over at the second last. He was just getting careless over his hurdles.'

Wing and a Prayer, who had been struggling in vain pursuit 100 yards behind, came through to win, to the delight of his jockey Simon Sherwood, who had only recently turned professional. It was the first time he had ridden against Desert Orchid and was hardly the ideal introduction to what was to become an invincible partnership.

Happily Desert Orchid escaped unscathed and now it really was time to turn his attention to steeplechasing. David Elsworth chose as his first race a minor event at Devon and Exeter, the windswept course high on Haldon Hill above Exeter. Desert Orchid started favourite at 5–4 on and the betting indicated that his only serious rival in a small field was another attractive grey, Charcoal Wally, who had begun his chasing career with a hard-earned success over Elsworth's mare, Allied Newcastle, at Kempton a fortnight earlier. Charcoal Wally, too, usually made the running but on this occasion he was quite unable to match Desert Orchid's jumping or galloping.

Brown remembers: 'He set off pretty quickly, shuffled to put himself right at the first fence and popped over like a sensible handicapper. He was quite brilliant. Really it was all very exciting.'

At the end of a memorable clear round Desert Orchid finished fully twenty-five lengths clear of Charcoal Wally. You could not possibly ask or expect to see a more impressive debut over fences and further runaway victories over stiffer fences at Ascot

An early example of the breathtaking jumping that was to make Desert Orchid a champion over fences

Just good friends, Desert Orchid and Colin Brown, winners of seventeen races together

(twice) and Sandown surely confirmed that the dashing grey was going to be even better over fences than hurdles.

Bold, arrogant, apparently carefree, Desert Orchid won his first four races over fences by an aggregate of sixty-four lengths, but at times he seemed almost too brave for his own good. David Elsworth now determined on an ambitious plan to bring him back to hurdles for just one run at Kempton in the Ladbroke Christmas Hurdle. Switching horses from fences to hurdles and back again is far more common in Ireland but here it is still regarded as highly unorthodox, even confusing, for hesitant jumpers. David Elsworth had no such qualms about Desert Orchid, but heavy rain over Christmas made the ground so soft that it was decided to withdraw him.

Steeplechasing, by its very nature, is a hazardous business and jump jockeys, sharing a common bond of danger and excitement, tend to be marvellously tough, cheerful and uncomplaining. You could not find a better example than Colin Brown.

Riding a hard-pulling, quick-jumping novice like Desert Orchid over unforgiving fences is not a matter for faint hearts. The risks involved are painfully obvious and jump jockeys know it is a matter of when rather than if they will be seriously hurt. More often than not the bad falls come in a novice chase and now Desert Orchid's winning sequence was about to be rudely interrupted at the downhill open ditch at Ascot in the appropriately named Thunder and Lightning Chase. It was the very fence that had ended the life of Killiney, a gentle giant of a horse who had promised so much over fences until his life was cruelly snuffed out.

Once again the race looked a formality though subsequent events were to prove that the winner, Pearlyman, would have been extremely hard to beat even if Desert Orchid had not ejected Colin Brown like a spent cartridge. The approach to the fifth fence on the run down to Swinley Bottom is covered with searing clarity for BBC television by a roving camera on a fast-moving car only yards from the runners on the inside of the running rail. Colin Brown remains convinced that it was the presence of the camera that led to his downfall.

'Going to the ditch he turned his head to the right and had a good look at the camera. I gave him a slap down the neck to make him concentrate and in two more strides we were at the fence,' he says.

Desert Orchid took off much too far outside the wings, landed on top of the ditch and flopped through the fence. Showing an instinct born of self-preservation, Colin Brown somehow survived this earthquake of a blunder but was then dislodged when Charcoal Wally jumped into the rear of Desert Orchid. Remarkably the grey still did not fall and could be seen galloping on gaily, jumping a few fences before allowing himself to be caught by Jackie Parrish in front of the stands. The only injury sustained by Colin Brown was to his pride.

Desert Orchid was, once again, odds-on to resume his winning run at Sandown in the Scilly Isles Novices' Chase but met his match in the mud-loving Berlin, who had previously won with impressive ease at Lingfield. The pair had a battle royal for most of the way, head to head, jumping the awkward railway fences side by side with breathtaking speed and accuracy, but hard as Desert Orchid tried he failed by half a length to overhaul Berlin on the final hill. Few would argue that jump racing was the major winner that day.

Once more Cheltenham beckoned and the chosen target at the 1986 Festival was the Arkle Challenge Trophy for novices over two miles. Desert Orchid ran his best race so far at the course but once again gave away ground by drifting and occasionally jumping right-handed. He was in front for most of the way but had no answer to the late charges of Oregon Trail and Charcoal Wally. Even so, in finishing third he was still thirteen lengths in front of Berlin.

Now David Elsworth decided to try him over half a mile further at Sandown. Back at his favourite racecourse he started at a shade of odds-on, but though leading to the last fence was unable to withstand the powerful finishing burst of Clara

As fine a sight as you could wish to see in chasing. Desert Orchid clears the fence in front of the packed stands in the Arkle Chase at Cheltenham

OVERLEAF: *Desert Orchid is hard pressed by Clara Mountain at the last fence at Sandown in March and is caught on the flat*

Mountain, who won by one and a half lengths. On the evidence of that run it would have been unfair to conclude that he did not stay two and a half miles.

Desert Orchid ran once more that season, again over two and a half miles, in a valuable novices' handicap at Ascot. Naturally he carried top weight of $11\frac{1}{2}$ stone but just for once he did not immediately surge off into the lead. He was in front, though, by the fourth fence but two mistakes in the closing stages sapped his strength and on the flat he was just run out of fourth place. It was the end of a busy campaign and he was giving 17 pounds or more in weight to the first three. No one could now be certain whether he truly stayed two and a half miles, let alone further. We would have to wait for another season to learn the answer to that intriguing question. One man already was in no doubt. His name was David Elsworth.

By this stage of Desert Orchid's career Simon Bullimore was readily acknowledging his good fortune in having a share in one of those rare horses that move the spirit. The deal that gave him 25 per cent of the grey was struck over dinner with his partner James Burridge ten years ago. Bullimore had just bought a new boat while Burridge was delighted with the progress of his yearling son of Flower Child. During a lively evening it was agreed that Burridge would join his friend on sailing holidays in the Mediterranean in exchange for a quarter share in the unknown young horse at a startlingly low price.

Bullimore recalls: 'We got caught in a frightful Mistral on our first trip in the Mediterranean and Jimmy swore he would never come sailing again so obviously I had the best end of the bargain. I was completely ignorant of racing at the time and thought my new horse would be going for the Derby and the Grand National.'

Jackie Parrish, meanwhile, was finding that looking after Desert Orchid was not always entirely pleasurable. After a particularly alarming experience on the all weather gallop she restricted her riding on him to walks and the shortest canters.

Jackie explains, 'He ran away with me straight over the end of the bank which quite put me off. But he knew what he had done and stopped which was just as well since I had no control.'

CHAPTER SEVEN

A surprise in the King George VI Chase

WHEN DESERT ORCHID first arrived at Whitsbury as a raw-boned three-year-old his colour was a dark shade of grey. Over the passage of years he became increasingly lighter.

Racehorses in training or at home invariably eat from a manger in the corner of their stable. The arrangements for Desert Orchid, of course, are different. He likes to know exactly what is going on outside in the yard at all times. Accordingly, his manger is hooked on the inside of his stable door so that he does not miss anything at meal times.

Jackie Parrish confirms, 'Above all he is a right old nosey parker.'

His diet is the same as other horses in training at Whitsbury: corn, horse nuts, carrots with chopped apple, hay and some damp bran. When the head lad Rodney Boult arrives, saddle in hand, and removes the horse's rug, there follows a familiar daily ritual. Desert Orchid kneels down in his box and enjoys a good old-fashioned roll, his legs pawing the air. Only then does he allow Rodney Boult to put on the saddle.

It is Boult, with God-given hands that can settle and relax the strongest puller, who invariably rides Desert Orchid at the head of the string each morning. The grey assumes his position in front as if by divine right. Should a stable companion impertinently attempt to join, or worse, pass him on the steep, winding narrow village lane that leads to the gallops, he will dart across, his ears laid back, and block him off by sheer physical intimidation. It is the same when the serious work of the day begins.

'I've never known a horse who loves to be in front so much,' says Rodney Boult admiringly.

Boult will tell you that Desert Orchid has learned to settle at home and is no longer a tearaway provided, of course, he is allowed to go in front. But on a golden morning at Whitsbury in the autumn of 1988 it seemed to me that the grey was almost winning the argument as he charged up the all-weather, imposing an intolerable strain on Rodney Boult's arms. Later, as he allowed Desert Orchid to have a pick of grass on the way

RIGHT & OPPOSITE: *A good old fashioned roll in his box before the serious business of the day. Rodney Boult waits patiently until Desert Orchid is ready to be saddled*

home, he admitted, 'Well he was a bit free this morning. He's usually keener than ever when he comes back after his holidays.'

Steeplechasers can sometimes be in training for three months or more before they are ready to race. This period is usually a little shorter for Desert Orchid because much of the obligatory walking and trotting on the roads to harden and strengthen legs, joints and muscles, is done by the Burridges before he returns to Whitsbury.

Certainly Desert Orchid was in outstanding form at home in the autumn of 1986 as he prepared for his first run at what seemed to be his favourite course, Sandown. The race chosen for him was the Holsten Export Lager Handicap Chase and since he had not won in his final five races in the spring he was undeniably well handicapped, receiving a massive 25 pounds from Very Promising, a horse he had beaten with ease over hurdles in the Kingwell Pattern Hurdle at Wincanton.

The formula was by now delightfully familiar. Eager to press on with the task, Desert Orchid raced away in front, jumping with breathtaking boldness, and stayed on to win as he liked. The distance of the race, significantly, was two and a half miles. No one could say now that he was simply a runaway speed horse.

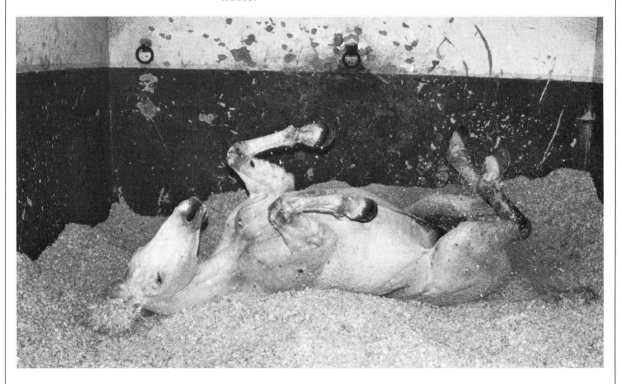

Desert Orchid performed well in defeat at Ascot next time, giving weight to the three horses who finished in front of him, then won decisively over two miles at the same course a fortnight before Christmas. There had been a time when it seemed Desert Orchid would fold up once headed in a race. Not any longer. At Ascot it was his old rival Charcoal Wally who forced the pace at halfway, but Desert Orchid was back in front two fences later and quickened clear in the finishing straight. You could not ask for a better indication of his continuing improvement over fences. At Cheltenham in the spring he had finished almost nine lengths behind Charcoal Wally. Now the same horse was twelve lengths behind him.

Desert Orchid (Rodney Boult) lead Barnbrook Again (Ross Arnott) on the gallops

The morning's work over, Desert Orchid and Rodney Boult saunter peacefully across the Hampshire downs

Up to this point Desert Orchid had been restricted to races over two or two and a half miles. His trainer now made the far-sighted decision to try him over three miles. Many people felt that the grey's free-running manner of racing would prevent him staying longer distances and were astonished when the trainer declared that Desert Orchid would run next in the King George VI Rank Chase at Kempton on Boxing Day, a championship race second only in importance to the

TOP: *A winning start to the new season at Sandown on 1 November 1986*

ABOVE: *Desert Orchid is clear over the last on his way to victory in the Frogmore Handicap Chase at Ascot on 13 December 1986*

Look no hands! Desert Orchid and Rodney Boult lead the string back to breakfast as David Elsworth walks alongside

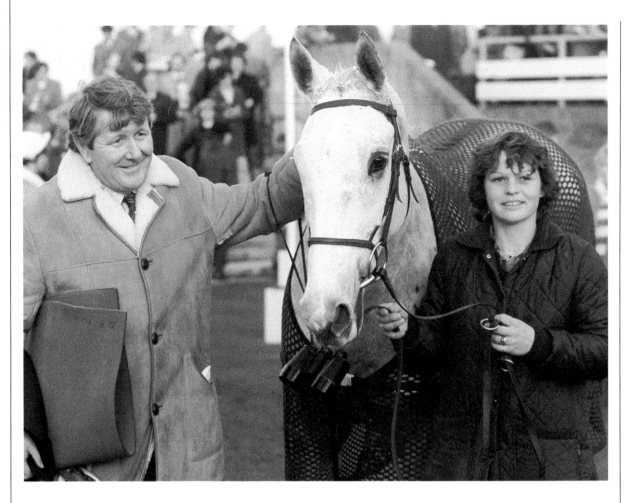

Cheltenham Gold Cup. Rodney Boult was one of those who questioned the grey's stamina.

'I just couldn't see him lasting. I felt the guv'nor was wrong,' he admits.

Bookmakers, too, dismissed Desert Orchid in the ante-post betting at 20–1. Elsworth, it seemed, was alone in his confidence but time was to confirm once more his acute perception of the horse's ability. He had told Desert Orchid's owners of his intention as long ago as the previous summer. When I asked a week before the race why he was taking a chance his reply was emphatic.

'I've always thought that the King George was made for Desert Orchid. Stay three miles? Of course he will. If the ground is good or fast he'll go off in front and set such a pace they won't catch him. He loves Kempton. I know you all think I'm mad running him but you wait and see.'

We could not say we had not been warned!

David Elsworth pauses to give the grey a well earned pat before going off to saddle another runner in the next race

A rare error as Desert Orchid flicks through the top of the fifth last fence on his way to a startling triumph in the King George VI Chase

David Elsworth's decision to run the grey in the King George VI Chase in addition to his stable companion Combs Ditch, left Colin Brown facing an agonising choice as he worked busily behind the bar of the Furze Bush in the days leading up to Christmas. Should he stay loyal to Desert Orchid, a horse with so much potential, or prefer Combs Ditch, who, with a bit of luck, might already have won the Kempton prize twice. A year earlier Combs Ditch had failed by a neck to overhaul Wayward Lad. Twelve months before that only a short head separated Combs Ditch from a famous victory over the mighty Burrough Hill Lad. Significantly, Colin Brown had ridden him on both occasions.

The jockey's dilemma was further complicated by an injury that had prevented Combs Ditch having a preliminary outing before the 1986 King George. But the old horse invariably ran well first time and was working impressively at Whitsbury. While Colin Brown contemplated his choice, David Elsworth

ABOVE & RIGHT: Well clear after the last but Simon Sherwood will not relax until the race is won. It is a dream first ride on Desert Orchid for the jockey

booked Simon Sherwood to ride the one which his stable jockey rejected.

Even on the morning of the race Colin Brown was still uncertain. Almost half an inch of rain had fallen over the Christmas holiday and when he reached Kempton he walked the course alone, hoping to find inspiration from the state of the ground. The fact that the going was extremely soft certainly influenced his decision. Richard Burridge helped, too, by assuring him he would be back on Desert Orchid next time whatever the result. So ninety minutes before the race, far from convinced he had picked the right one, Colin Brown opted for Combs Ditch. The betting suggested he had made a wise choice. Combs Ditch was steady in the market as second favourite at 4–1, while punters wishing to back Desert Orchid found 20–1 and 16–1 freely available.

The jockey who rode Desert Orchid for the first time at Kempton was Simon Edward Harlakenden Sherwood, son of a wealthy landowner, old boy of Radley and twice amateur champion jockey before turning professional in August, 1985. A quiet, sympathetic, stylish rider, he was to prove an ideal choice, but at Kempton he wanted to be on Combs Ditch.

'Well,' he explains, 'to be honest I thought he looked the safer conveyance. I had not studied Desert Orchid but I had this image of a hairy thing that used to tear off in front. You have to remember that few people, apart from the trainer, believed Desert Orchid would stay three miles. I was slightly anxious that he would go flying off in front at a million miles an hour and fall in a heap after two miles. That was my image of the horse.'

It was an unlikely prelude to one of the great partnerships in the history of steeplechasing.

Jackie Parrish collects a voucher for a free holiday

OPPOSITE: Simon Sherwood, James Burridge and Jane Elsworth receive their prizes from the Queen Mother

Colin Brown soon knew his fate. Combs Ditch, like a boxer having his first fight after a long break, was woefully ring-rusty and scrambled uneasily over the first two fences at the rear. By then Desert Orchid, setting his customary scorching gallop, had already gone beyond recall.

Simon Sherwood recalls: 'Desert Orchid was quite fantastic that day and I never saw another horse in the race near us. I think perhaps the other jockeys felt he would not last. They were riding their own races and ignoring us in front, just waiting for us to come back.'

Just as David Elsworth had predicted, the soggy ground and the extra distance failed to disturb Desert Orchid's relentless galloping, soaring jumping and matchless enthusiasm. The chasing group moved a little closer on the final bend but another towering leap by Desert Orchid at the second-last fence gained precious yards and he sailed cheerfully home in splendid isolation, fully fifteen lengths clear of his closest pursuer, Door Latch. David Elsworth missed some of the celebrations as he ran down the course to help administer oxygen to Combs Ditch, who was exhausted by the time Colin Brown pulled him up in the straight when the cause was hopeless. Happily the horse recovered quickly and the jockey took the reverse with typical good nature.

When the trainer returned from ministering to Combs Ditch he paid his jockey a glowing tribute.

'We all feel sorry for Colin. He has been a great influence on Desert Orchid's career and has been the main contributor to the horse's confidence.'

Elsworth added, 'I could not understand why everyone else dismissed Desert Orchid's chance without a second glance. In the end I thought I might be losing my touch. Perhaps everyone will believe me now.'

Jackie Parrish was not forgotten as those closest to Desert Orchid stepped up to receive their awards from the smiling Queen Mother, jump racing's finest supporter. Jackie's prize was a two-week holiday from the race sponsors, Rank.

OPPOSITE: *Whatever the weather Desert Orchid always leads his stable companions at home*

CHAPTER EIGHT

'A heart as big as himself'

T HE WHEEL OF FORTUNE can turn viciously in jump racing and twenty-four hours after his heady triumph in the King George, Simon Sherwood was on his way to hospital by ambulance after the most horrible fall imaginable at Kempton. Somehow Simon managed to survive the blunder that sent his mount, Drive on Jimmy, lurching towards the ground, but he was left hanging perilously round the horse's neck and his frantic efforts to hang on merely brought the horse crashing down onto him. The hapless jockey became tangled in the horse's breastplate

and was kicked in the head and back as Drive on Jimmy trampled on him. His injuries were diagnosed as severe concussion and bruising and, most serious, crushed vertebrae in his back. Such are the daily hazards facing the brave men who so cheerfully risk their lives in the name of sport.

Desert Orchid's swashbuckling triumph in the King George VI Chase had caught the imagination of the racing public and he was the centre of attention for his next race, the Gainsborough Chase, again over three miles at Sandown, where he was

Another bold leap ensures victory for Desert Orchid in the Gainsborough Handicap Chase at Sandown in February 1987

Exercising in the snow is fun for horses

re-united with Colin Brown. Fully aware of the dangers of allowing him to steal too much lead, the other jockeys this time tried to stay in touch but the result was the same. Carrying 11 stone 10 pounds and conceding lumps of weight all round, Desert Orchid won with supreme ease, sweeping his earnings from first-prize money past £100,000. So to Wincanton, where his annual warm-up for Cheltenham in the Jim Ford Challenge Cup proved to be a majestic exhibition of jumping. Way, way behind, almost two fences in arrears, was the weary figure of West Tip, winner of the Seagram Grand National ten months earlier.

Inevitably people began to press for the increasingly popular grey to run in the Cheltenham Gold Cup, steeplechasing's premier championship, but his name was not among the entries for the 1987 race. Richard Burridge explained at the time, 'None of us, including the trainer and jockey, have ever been keen on running him in the Gold Cup.' It was a statement we were to hear repeatedly in the following twelve months before David Elsworth began to press for a change of plan.

Desert Orchid was defeated again at the Cheltenham Festival but this time, at least, there was no need to look for excuses after his excellent and close third behind Pearlyman and Very Promising, in the Queen Mother Champion Chase over two miles. He led, as usual, jumping fluently, but the old weakness of drifting right-handed cost him valuable ground, particularly on landing over the second last fence.

Jackie Parrish leads out Desert Orchid for the last time in the 1987 Whitbread Gold Cup

Out in front as usual. Desert Orchid and Colin Brown on their way to winning the Jim Ford Chase at Wincanton on 26 February 1987

Pearlyman, the 13–8 favourite, and Very Promising immediately dashed through the welcoming gap and opened up a useful lead over Desert Orchid. The first two raced side by side all the way up the final testing hill to the line, but it was noticeable that Desert Orchid, running up the centre of the course, was making ground again in the final 100 yards. At the finish the grey was only just over three lengths away in third place behind the narrow winner, Pearlyman. It was clear by now, beyond any reasonable doubt, that Desert Orchid was markedly more effective on a right-handed course.

David Elsworth concluded: 'It is very apparent Cheltenham does not suit him, though I don't know why. Probably most horses have a preference one way or another. His is more pronounced. He is only 75 per cent round Cheltenham but if they ran the Gold Cup at Kempton he would win it four years in a row.'

Desert Orchid's remarkable victory in the Peregrine Handicap Chase three weeks later over two and a half miles was the one that convinced David Elsworth that he could win the Gold Cup despite his natural preference for right-handed courses. The grey appeared to face a hopelessly daunting task with a welter burden of 12 stone 4 pounds at Ascot on going made impossibly soft by overnight rain. Anyone doubting the effect of weight on a horse's back should pop round to the local grocer, buy 14 pounds of potatoes, hoist them onto their shoulders, and try running uphill for a mile or two. Certainly Desert Orchid needed all his undoubted qualities of courage and resolution to regain the lead from Gold Bearer who, in comparison, was carrying the feather weight of 9 stone 8 pounds.

Concession of similar weights at times proved too much even for the peerless Arkle and when Gold Bearer surged into a clear lead on the final bend, not even the grey's most fervent supporters could have anticipated what was to happen next. Gold Bearer did not stop but slowly, obstinately, wonderfully, Desert Orchid fought his way back into contention, took a narrow advantage at the final fence and raced gallantly home for a most improbable triumph.

Colin Brown reflects, 'That race stands out in my mind as one of his greatest performances. It showed his heart was as big as himself.'

David Elsworth chose the Whitbread Gold Cup at Sandown as Desert Orchid's final race of the season. The distance this time was three miles, five furlongs and eighteen yards, infinitely further than he had ever raced before. The ground had dried up to firm and in the days leading up to the race it was discovered that Desert Orchid was suffering from corns. Athletes will tell

A fond farewell from Jackie Parrish to the horse she had looked after with such devotion

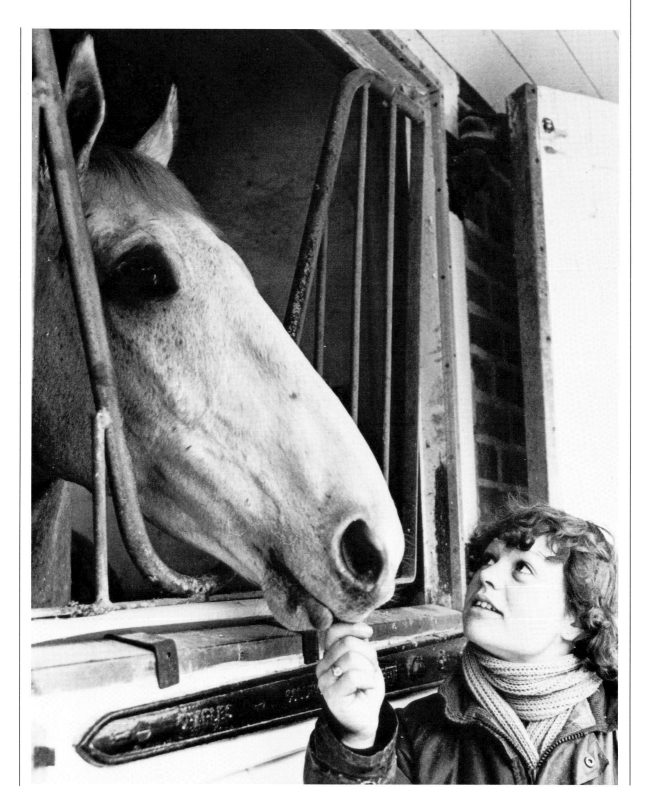

you that it is bad enough *running* on corns; jumping on them is considerably more painful and although the troublesome corn was removed, and the horse's feet packed with ice the night before the race, it is possible that his front feet were still sore when he raced at Sandown.

By this stage of his career Desert Orchid had a large and vociferous fan club of his own at Sandown but those who gathered on the Esher slopes to honour him were to be disappointed. For once his handsome grey head was not to be seen at the head of the race at any stage and after two uncharacteristic mistakes in the back straight Colin Brown pulled him up a mile from the finish. The race was won deservedly and excitingly by the unpronounceable Lean Ar Aghaidh and his dashing young jockey Guy Landau, who together had given an effervescent display of jumping in leading the Grand National field a merry dance until the flat three weeks earlier.

Colin Brown reports: 'Desert Orchid had his ears back that day and was not at all happy on the ground. I think we all knew it was not his true running. The important thing was that he seemed all right afterwards.' Despite that rare reverse Desert Orchid was chosen as Horse of the Year by a panel of leading racing journalists.

By now Colin Brown and his partner had sold the Furze Bush and in the summer of 1987 Colin became landlord of the Ibex, a cosy country pub at Chaddleworth that was soon to become a favourite haunt of racing people from the Lambourn valley.

CHAPTER NINE

Rash tactics and a new jockey

T HE FACT THAT Desert Orchid was fit and able to return into training once more in the autumn of 1987 for his sixth consecutive season was a remarkable testimony to his conformation. One of the reasons so many racegoers prefer jumping to flat racing is the delight of greeting seasoned hurdlers and chasers year after year like old and trusted friends. In marked contrast flat horses, particularly the best ones, tend to race only a handful of times before being rushed off to stud with indecent haste like guests at a party who barely have time for a handshake before leaving.

Most jumpers, particularly chasers, miss a season or two after operations to repair leg injuries caused by the strain and stress on joints and tendons from racing on all types of ground. Firm going, particularly, damages legs of horses jumping and galloping at speed. Corns apart, Desert Orchid seems to have avoided these problems. He has always been a wonderfully sound horse, which is perhaps surprising for such a carefree, extravagant jumper, though he is close to the ideal size and shape, with good clean limbs.

'He is so beautifully well balanced to sit on,' says Rodney Boult admiringly.

The pattern for the grey's annual summer holiday was by now well established. After a well-deserved break at grass in Leicestershire he would spend six weeks or so with Richard Burridge at his remote home high on the moors in North Yorkshire, walking and trotting on the steep roads each morning to harden and strengthen his legs.

Burridge has gradually emerged as the spokesman for Desert Orchid. Tall, distinctive, at times introspective, he is a script writer, responsible for such recent films as *The Fourth Protocol* and *Absolute Beginners*. He lives a solitary existence and the responsibility of owning such a famous horse at times seems to rest heavily on him. The teasing agony of anticipation, indeed expectation of continuing success is heightened by the ready awareness of the very real risks to Desert Orchid each time he is

Preparing for the long season ahead: Desert Orchid ridden by Clare Pears on a quiet road in North Yorkshire

Richard Burridge working at home in the study of his home high on the North Yorkshire Moors

led out onto the racecourse. Richard Burridge is an exceptionally generous owner and always makes it clear that his first priority is the horse's welfare. Hence his acute anxiety in the hours before the Cheltenham Gold Cup.

'I do pray a lot for this horse,' he reveals. 'The most important thing in each race is that he comes back safely.'

When Desert Orchid returned to Whitsbury in the autumn of 1987 it was into the tender care of a pretty but tiny stable girl, Janice Coyle, one of the longest serving members of David Elsworth's team. Jackie Parrish, who adored Desert Orchid, and had looked after him so lovingly, had married earlier in the year. Stable lads' hours are long and often unsociable, particularly at weekends. Soon after her marriage Jackie decided, with

New friends. Desert Orchid and his new lass Janice Coyle

Yet another winning start to the season. Desert Orchid soars gracefully over the water at Wincanton on his way to an impressive victory in the Terry Biddlecombe Chase in October 1987

some reluctance, to leave racing. She still lives in the village of Whitsbury and now works in a butcher's shop in nearby Fordingbridge.

Janice Coyle, a tidy little rider, won three races as an apprentice jockey from severely limited chances. Two of those victories came in consecutive runnings of the Florence Nagle Girls' Apprentice Handicap at Kempton, the race founded by the forthright veteran campaigner who did so much to force the Jockey Club to allow women to hold training licences.

When Janice Coyle leads up Desert Orchid at the racecourse she always wears the sweater knitted for her by her mother in the familiar Burridge dark blue and grey colours with the horse's name on the back. In August 1988, soon after winning a race at Chepstow on Elsworth's Mo Ceri, Janice received a dozen bottles of champagne for being named Lanson Lady of the Month. She also looks after two other horses each day but understandably events of the past two years have made Desert Orchid her favourite.

'Being with him tends to make you the centre of attention,' she says. Standing beside him in the box Janice seems barely big or strong enough to groom and handle such a fine, imposing thoroughbred, but they clearly have a strong and happy working relationship.

'He's never nasty but can be a bit fidgety and impatient,' she adds. 'And sometimes he does not like being brushed under his tummy.'

As the Desert Orchid legend has developed, more and more people come to see and touch him at the races and many bring cards and presents for the horse and his attendant.

Janice Coyle's first outing with Desert Orchid ended in triumph. The grey's runaway victory in the Terry Biddlecombe Chase at Wincanton on his seasonal debut at the end of October 1987 confirmed that six years' hard work had clearly not affected his uninhibited zest for racing. No matter that he was meeting markedly inferior horses. He did not know that. He was impatient as ever at the start, soon held a decisive lead and won unchallenged by a distance. It was the same story next time at

There's not a lot of room to spare as Desert Orchid brushes over a ditch at Kempton in the Rank Boxing Day Trial

Colin Brown's last success on Desert Orchid in the same race. It's a memory to last a lifetime

Kempton in the Rank Boxing Day Trial Chase, an ideal race over two and a half miles that could not have suited him better if David Elsworth had drawn up the conditions. Though he did not know it at the time it was to be the last occasion Colin Brown experienced the exhilaration of victory on Desert Orchid. No one was more delighted at Kempton than the clerk of the course, Michael Webster, who revealed that the presence of the grey had increased the attendance by 50 per cent.

The handicapper, however, was inevitably setting jump racing's most popular chaser increasingly severe tasks and Desert Orchid suffered a rare defeat at his favourite course, Sandown, when narrowly failing to concede 2 stone to the prolific two-mile chaser Long Engagement. David Elsworth commented, 'I hate seeing him beaten but his two wins this season have been too easy and he needed a good work-out to put him right for the King George.'

In 1986 the presence of Desert Orchid in the King George VI Rank Chase had been dismissed as a whim of David Elsworth. He was ignored in the betting and by the tipsters in the build-up to the race. What a difference a year makes. In 1987 Desert Orchid was a red-hot favourite at evens to triumph again, but those of us who had long believed in the invincibility of British steeplechasing were given serious cause to reconsider that traditional view as the French-trained Nupsala took the prize with damning authority.

Nupsala truly was the avenger of Waterloo. Overlooked in the ante-post betting at a derisory 50–1, he beat the very best we could muster with alarming ease. The lengthy odds were

perhaps understandable since a French chaser had not won in this country for twenty-five years. With three front runners in the race, the pace was always going to be fast but no one, I suspect, believed that Desert Orchid, Beau Ranger and Cybrandian would set off quite as quickly as they did. Peter Scudamore on Beau Ranger, in particular, seemed determined to disappoint the favourite at all costs. Colin Brown naturally felt justified in trying to ward him off. Somehow horses and riders were still intact after negotiating the first four fences at a speed

Desert Orchid pricks his ears as he surveys his audience after winning at Kempton

you would not normally see even in a flat-race sprint, but the early suicidal dash of the leading trio surely ended any chance of their winning. They simply ran themselves into the ground.

Cybrandian fell at the fourteenth fence, and Peter Scudamore's attempt to disappoint Desert Orchid rebounded as Beau Ranger dropped back exhausted soon afterwards. The grey, remarkably, was still in front on the final turn but it was only on sufferance. Just behind him Nupsala was galloping with unmistakable ease. The Frenchman moved smoothly into the

The pace in the King George VI Chase is already much too fierce as Cybrandian (left), Beau Ranger (centre) and Desert Orchid soar over the second fence

lead on the run to the second last and was fully in command when Forgive 'N' Forget fell heavily at the final fence, leaving Desert Orchid to finish a weary second, fifteen lengths behind the unexpected winner. Colin Brown conceded afterwards: 'I thought Nupsala looked like a bit of a cart horse at the start but he could certainly run. I couldn't believe my eyes when he came cruising past.'

The rash tactics of the jockeys on the three front runners undoubtedly played into the hands of the French winner and

given the chance again Colin Brown, I suspect, would not allow himself to be drawn into the argument from the start. He has always maintained that Desert Orchid does not have to make the running.

Desert Orchid was given a short rest after his hard race at Kempton and did not appear again until the Gainsborough Chase at Sandown on 6 February. The judges in the paddock chose him as the best turned out horse and so Janice Coyle added a further prize to her growing collection. Another of Elsworth's owners, Juliette Reed, wanted her horse Rhyme 'N' Reason to run in the same race. Both were beaten by the well-handicapped Charter Party. Time was to show that Desert Orchid was attempting the impossible in giving 17 pounds to Charter Party. The grey ran his usual honest race from the front but he was passed at the last fence by Charter Party and was also overtaken in the shadow of the winning post by Rhyme 'N' Reason, who was receiving 21 pounds.

PREVIOUS PAGE: *Desert Orchid and Run and Skip in unison at the sixth last fence in the Gainsborough Handicap Chase at Sandown in February 1988*

At the last Charter Party is just in front and pulls clear on the flat

There were times in the 1987–8 season when David Elsworth wondered if the grey star of his stable was quite at his sparkling best. But when you consider that within a few weeks Charter Party won the Tote Cheltenham Gold Cup and Rhyme 'N' Reason triumphed in the Seagram Grand National it is hard to fault Desert Orchid's performance that day at Sandown. Certainly Colin Brown believed the horse was showing positive signs of returning to his best form. Even so, Desert Orchid's return to another of his favoured tracks, Wincanton, was not a particularly happy one and surprisingly he was outpaced on the run-in by Kildimo, a very good horse on his day but an inconsistent one.

Such is the curious nature of steeplechasing that Desert Orchid has since been elevated to the status of a National hero while Kildimo has failed to win another race.

One of the major regrets of Rodney Boult's long and deeply rewarding association with Desert Orchid is that he has not once

Rodney Boult is not in sight as Desert Orchid is led out at Wincanton

been present at the races on a day when the grey has won. Boult was at Cheltenham when Desert Orchid ran unaccountably badly in the Champion Hurdle and he was at Kempton when he fell over hurdles with a race at his mercy. Other visits to see him run at Kempton, Cheltenham and Ascot proved equally fruitless. Was he putting a jinx on the horse? Some of the lads certainly thought so and since most of Desert Orchid's races are on television, the head lad resolved, reluctantly, to remain an armchair viewer in future.

What is life, however, without temptation? That day at Wincanton no one connected with the horse envisaged defeat. What's more, the course was only an hour's gentle drive from Whitsbury. Rodney Boult had time to finish his morning's work, dash to the races and still be back in time for evening stables. This time he made sure his plans were a closely guarded secret, arrived at Wincanton in disguise, kept well out of the way of anyone who might recognise him and watched in dismay as Kildimo sprinted past Desert Orchid on the short run-in.

He recalls: 'I could not believe my eyes. I thought the horse was a certainty that day.'

Rodney Boult left the course deeply depressed. What, he wondered, had he done to inflict such bad fortune on Desert

Kildimo catches Desert Orchid at the last fence at Wincanton on 25 February, much to the dismay of Rodney Boult watching in disguise from the stand

Orchid? That evening Richard Burridge rang him to commiserate and mentioned that one or two people were sure they had spotted the head lad in the distance at Wincanton. Boult's cover was blown.

He confirms: 'After that nothing would drag me away from here to watch him at the races.'

Rodney Boult has one other regret. 'You know he's such a beautiful horse to ride, with such a spring in his step, I'd give anything to sit on him over fences in a race. Anything.' It is an ambition, however, he knows will never be fulfilled.

While Rodney Boult continued to dream of the intense pleasure of riding Desert Orchid over fences, the man who had been his jockey from the very start was contemplating retirement. The 1988 Cheltenham Festival proved a supremely emotional one for Colin Brown. Business at the Ibex was flourishing and he was preparing to take over the tenancy of a second pub, the Wheatsheaf, at Chilton Foliat, near Hungerford. He no longer had the appetite or time to justify driving 200

RIGHT & BELOW: The last time together for Desert Orchid and Colin Brown. They are as fluent as ever but once more are beaten at Cheltenham

miles or more for one modest spare ride at a distant race meeting. Early in January he determined to retire at the Festival. Despite the temptation to continue while Desert Orchid was racing, it was a grown-up, sensible decision. Too many jump jockeys go on too long, often with painful, even disastrous results, because they know only racing and cannot believe anything can match the thrill of riding over fences at speed. But there is life after riding and with a young family to support and a business already established Colin Brown felt it was the right moment to give up.

Colin began his final Cheltenham as a jockey with a shocking fall on Sir Blake at the final hurdle in the Sun Alliance Novices' Hurdle. Sir Blake was on the heels of the leaders and travelling strongly when he nose-dived heavily. Subsequent events suggested he might well have won. Luckily horse and rider escaped unhurt and Colin ran back to pull on Desert Orchid's colours for the final time. Once again they were trying to win the Queen Mother Champion Chase and once again they were defeated by Pearlyman, this time by five lengths.

Colin reflects: 'Naturally I badly wanted to win on him that day but he ran a great race in defeat. He jumped like a stag, flew the last and stayed on well.'

Ideally Colin Brown would have liked to retire then and there. But he had been booked by Brooke Sanders several weeks in advance for Calapaez in the *Daily Express* Triumph Hurdle on Thursday and did not want to let her down. He told Richard Burridge and David Elsworth of his decision just before going out to ride Calapaez, who finished tenth. After the race Brown announced his retirement in an interview with me on BBC television.

David Elsworth paid his jockey the warmest possible tribute: 'Whoever rides for me, I will never find anybody more loyal or with more integrity than Colin. We have had some marvellous times together,' he said.

Colin Brown rode a total of 292 winners. Seventeen of them came on Desert Orchid, who he describes with admirable clarity as 'A once-in-a-lifetime horse'. Since his retirement Colin has opened the Orchid bar at the Ibex, which naturally enough displays many photos of his enduring partnership with the flying grey. With two pubs to organise, Colin Brown is busier than ever but whenever Desert Orchid runs the landlord takes time off to go to support his old comrade.

The departure of Colin Brown left Desert Orchid briefly without a jockey for his next race, the Chivas Regal Cup at the Liverpool Grand National meeting early in April. There was only one logical choice as successor. Simon Sherwood.

CHAPTER TEN

The splendour of Liverpool and the Whitbread Gold Cup

SIMON SHERWOOD was so small at school when he was fifteen that it was arranged for him to become an apprentice on the flat with the celebrated Newmarket trainer, the late Sam Armstrong.

He confirms: 'Lester Piggott was my hero and my wall was covered with his photos. I thought jumping was a waste of time in those days.' Much to his father's relief, he then began to grow and so his education followed a more conventional route from Radley to a three-year course at the Royal Agricultural College at Cirencester.

Life on the family farm beckoned, but his elder brother Oliver had been supremely successful as an amateur jockey before becoming a racehorse trainer in Lambourn and Simon, too, was drawn irresistibly to racing, initially as an assistant to Tom Jones and then Gavin Pritchard-Gordon, both flat trainers in Newmarket. Riding in point-to-points then set him firmly on the path to becoming a professional jockey.

The presence of Beau Ranger in the small field for the Chivas Regal Cup suggested another furious, frenetic confrontation with Desert Orchid, but it did not happen because Beau Ranger lost one of his racing plates on the way to the start and was withdrawn at the last moment. His absence allowed Desert Orchid to dominate in his customary regal manner. Showing only brief glimpses of his much publicised bias against left-hand courses, the grey skipped gaily round the tight turns, was already in control entering the final straight and stayed on splendidly to foil Kildimo's belated challenge by a most comfortable margin of eight lengths. It was his first success on a left-handed course at the ninth attempt.

Simon Sherwood was ecstatic. He reported: 'My only anxious moment came when the saddle-cloth began to slip in the closing stages. Colin had done all the hard work and I just had to sit on. The least I owe him is a large dinner.'

There was an amusing postscript to Desert Orchid's first success at Liverpool. The celebrations, as you would expect,

LEFT & BELOW: *Two fascinating studies of Desert Orchid crossing the only Grand National fence in the Chivas Regal Cup, the water, as he wins for the first time left-handed at Aintree*

continued long and hard into the evening at the course. Richard Burridge slipped away for a few minutes to let his dogs out of his jeep for a run over the vast expanse of Aintree. Imagine his horror when he found that they had already escaped into the darkness. A long, fruitless search followed and at some stage Burridge drove over to seek solace at a party in full swing at the Post House Hotel at Haydock. Later still, he returned to the racecourse shortly before dawn and eventually found, to his profound relief, the exhausted hounds.

It proved to be a supremely successful meeting for David

The field is tightly packed behind the grey leader at an early stage in the 1988 Whitbread Gold Cup

Elsworth. Rhyme 'N' Reason gained a remarkable victory in the Seagram Grand National after virtually falling at Becher's Brook on the first circuit and Sir Blake rounded off a memorable week with a crushing success in the final race of National day.

For the few hectic days that followed at Whitsbury, jump racing's most popular horse was not, for once, the centre of attention. A handful of visitors paused to acknowledge his presence as he leaned his head over his door wondering at all the fuss. But most were only concerned with admiring Rhyme 'N' Reason at the other end of the stable yard. Soon Rhyme 'N'

Desert Orchid lands a fraction in front of Kildimo over the last fence

Reason left for treatment to his hock, injured almost certainly as he scrambled to his feet at Becher's, and Desert Orchid was once more the undisputed star of the show.

David Elsworth and Richard Burridge both felt that Desert Orchid deserved a second chance in the Whitbread Gold Cup at the end of April, but again corns interrupted his preparation in the week before the race. The trainer even issued a statement on the grey's condition on the eve of the race and added that despite his corns the horse had not missed a day's work.

Rodney Boult noticed something was wrong with Desert Orchid's action five days before the Whitbread. When the horse's shoes were removed a small corn was discovered. Twice-daily laser treatment and constant poulticing failed to heal the problem and so Elsworth and his vet, Jan Puzio, decided to exercise Desert Orchid without shoes. To avoid the chance of bruising or further damage to his sore feet the horse was kept from the roads and taken to and from the gallops by horsebox. When the stable's blacksmith, Paul Henderson, gently fitted Desert Orchid's racing plates on Saturday morning he placed special rubber pads under them.

David Elsworth particularly was more anxious about the horse's feet than his ability to last the extreme distance of the Whitbread Gold Cup, fully three miles, five furlongs and eighteen yards.

OPPOSITE AND OVERLEAF: *Neck and neck. Three superb action photographs of Desert Orchid and Kildimo locked together as they start the final climb to the winning post*

'Oh yes, he'll stay all right,' he assured me in an interview in the *Sunday Express*. 'He goes on and on. He's not a softie and he loves a battle. Really the extra distance is only three or four good leaps.'

Despite his unrivalled record over the Sandown course Desert Orchid drifted out to 6–1 in the betting before the Whitbread Gold Cup. Perhaps his well-publicised corns unnerved some punters. Others did not share Elsworth's faith in the horse's stamina. With corns on his feet and wings on his heels, Desert Orchid answered all the doubts with a glorious, emotional victory in the sunshine at Sandown. He bounded away in front when the tapes rose, and though headed briefly twice, was ahead once more on the run back to the pond fence, three from home. His old rival Kildimo posed a serious threat approaching the final fence but another majestic leap secured the prize for Desert Orchid and on the uphill climb he ran clear again without Simon Sherwood as much as feeling for his whip.

'The last thing Desert Orchid wants is to be bullied,' reported Simon. 'He's the one that likes to do the bullying!'

Kildimo was magnificent in defeat but quite simply he was beaten by a better and braver horse, who showed not the slightest

OPPOSITE: *The veins standing out on Desert Orchid's neck in the sunshine offer vivid testimony of his supreme effort to reach the line first*

evidence of the foot trouble that had given those closest to him such sleepless nights all week. No one would ever dare suggest again that Desert Orchid did not stay. No wonder David Elsworth had tears in his eyes as he greeted the bravest of all greys. In truth there was scarcely a dry eye in the house as he returned to a spontaneous, heartfelt and prolonged ovation from the enormous crowd. Elsworth knew better than anyone that only the most delicate and constant care had enabled Desert Orchid to meet his date with destiny.

'He only just got here with the help of our vet, blacksmith, some laser treatment and an awful lot of prayers,' he confirmed of the horse whose victory ensured his first trainers' championship.

Everyone's racehorse of the year. Desert Orchid in the summer of 1988

Once again, in his moment of triumph, Richard Burridge made it clear that the Cheltenham Gold Cup was not likely to be part of Desert Orchid's programme the following season. 'It is a course which tends to punish mistakes more than reward brilliance. I just don't think it is the right race for him,' he said.

Events were to change his mind.

Desert Orchid's exploits at Liverpool and Sandown ensured that he was once again the undisputed National Hunt Champion in a vote organised by the Racegoers' Club. His total of first-prize money had risen by the end of the season to £189,687. Only three horses, Dawn Run, Wayward Lad and Burrough Hill Lad, had won more and he was to pass them all within a year.

Soon after the Whitbread Gold Cup Simon Sherwood met Arkle's jockey, Pat Taaffe, in Ireland. The tall, quiet-spoken Irishman was lavish in his praise of Desert Orchid. Simon recalls: 'Pat said he was very glad this horse was not around in his day because he believes he would have given Arkle a really good race.'

There could be no possible higher praise.

CHAPTER ELEVEN

'The best horse in the country'

On the moors in late summer 1988, Desert Orchid (Clare Pears) with his half-sister Peacework (ridden by Richard Burridge) and Trailing Rose

JANE ELSWORTH, naturally one of Desert Orchid's most devoted admirers, approached four major bookmakers in the autumn of 1988 with an ambitious project for a charitable cause close to her heart. Since Jane is delightfully persuasive, all four agreed to donate £50 to the Great Ormond Street Wishing-Well Appeal every time Desert Orchid ran in the 1988–9 season. They further offered a £50 free bet on him in each race. It was to prove a highly profitable deal for the Appeal fund.

Whenever Desert Orchid goes racing the man in charge of his every move is 52–year-old Peter Maughan, a quiet, efficient, totally reliable stableman who was travelling head lad for Arthur Budgett in the Derby-winning days of Blakeney and Morston. When Budgett's successor, James Bethell, moved to Whitsbury, Maughan went with him and later joined David Elsworth.

The travelling head lad is a most vital part of a trainer's team. He will ensure that the box leaves the yard on time, that horses are properly bandaged and protected for the journey ahead. On arrival at the course he will declare the runners for the afternoon, check the stabling arrangements and more often than not help saddle horses before their races and wash them down afterwards. He is, in short, bag carrier, adviser, nurse and servant, on call twenty-four hours a day. Peter Maughan has supervised a thousand and more winners. Few, if any, he says have matched the intelligence of Desert Orchid.

'Oh, he's a right show off and loves an audience. You can see him light up and rise to the occasion when we take him into the paddock. He pricks his ears and walks around as if he is King. What he does not like is people crowding around him particularly after a race. When it happens he'll normally stop until they give him a bit of space.'

After his usual pre-season conditioning on the hilly roads near Richard Burridge's Yorkshire home, Desert Orchid returned to Whitsbury in outstanding form. From the moment he started cantering he seemed to be trying to pull Rodney Boult's arms from their sockets.

One morning in September 1988, Simon Sherwood, showing exceptional early-season keenness, volunteered to ride Desert Orchid at exercise. It was the first and last time he was to make such a request. When the grey set off, up the shavings canter, it was clear his jockey was experiencing considerable discomfort.

Simon recalls: 'Suddenly he took a stronger grip and for the next furlong and a half he was seriously "trapping". I admit he almost bolted with me. I was not entirely in control.'

David Elsworth, who had an inkling of what might happen,

Poetry in motion in the autumn sunshine. Desert Orchid leaps thrillingly over the water at Wincanton in October 1988

was watching events a little further along the all-weather surface. He walked over to the edge of the shavings with Polos in his outstretched hand, called out and at once the horse slowed, with his ears pricked mischievously.

Desert Orchid's seventh and unrivalled campaign as a race-horse opened at the end of October on a golden afternoon at Wincanton. The opposition was modest enough in the Terry

Biddlecombe Chase but that made no difference to the dashing grey's style of racing. He sprinted off at the start, was soon a distance clear, jumping like a gazelle, saved one of his most spectacular leaps for the last and galloped past the packed stands to rapturous aplause.

Again Richard Burridge hinted that his horse might miss the Gold Cup in March in favour of a shorter race at Cheltenham.

Unseasonably fast going at Kempton in mid-November worried David Elsworth sufficiently to withdraw Desert Orchid from the Boxing Day Trial Chase ninety minutes before the race. With only two opponents, who appeared outclassed, the

A day off for Desert Orchid because the ground is too firm at Kempton on 16 November, but he is paraded in front of the stands flanked by Peter Maughan and Janice Coyle

Desert Orchid as flamboyant as ever takes off well away from the ditch as Panto Prince adopts a more *cautious approach in the Tingle Creek Handicap at Sandown*

prize of almost £10,000 seemed at the grey's mercy, but the trainer made his decision without regret after walking the course.

Although a large crowd had gathered to see Desert Orchid at the midweek meeting, no one could reasonably criticise the trainer for not wishing to risk damaging the horse's legs on ground that was extremely firm. He had left him in at the overnight stage, hoping in vain for some late rain to ease the jar in the ground. Elsworth was fined a statutory £70 for withdrawing the horse, who was then paraded in front of the stands flanked by Janice Coyle and Peter Maughan.

Simon Sherwood's luck changed dramatically when he

Out on his own now as he defies the handicapper in the most exciting manner at Sandown

TOP: *Another lightning jump gains Desert Orchid valuable ground from Vodkatini in the King George VI Chase at Kempton on Boxing Day 1988*

ABOVE: *Desert Orchid lands safely over the last in front of Kildimo on his way to his second victory in the race*

A happy group with Desert Orchid who seems more interested in the cameraman

returned to Wincanton on 19 November. He fell heavily, twice in ninety minutes, and was rushed to hospital after the second fall when his mount Patrico crashed horrifically through a swinging hurdle. Battered, shaken and concussed, the jockey also cracked two of his back teeth and was now involved in a race against time for his next appointment with Desert Orchid in the Tingle Creek Handicap Chase at Sandown on 3 December. Jump jockeys are a remarkably resilient breed of men and though it would be true to say he felt less than perfect, Simon Sherwood declared himself fit to ride at Sandown with twenty-four hours to spare. Ironically, the manner of his come-back ride on The Milroy aroused the interest of the stewards, but he had a much happier experience on Desert Orchid the next day.

He confirms: 'Just the thought of this horse speeds your recovery up a bit. Naturally you feel a bit possessive towards a horse like him and you don't like the thought of someone else sitting on his back. Desert Orchid was in a real bullish mood that day and David was convinced he would win.' The jockey,

A heartfelt kiss from Janice Coyle as the grey nuzzles Richard Burridge

for once, was pessimistic about having to give so much weight away to specialist two-mile chasers and feared they might bustle the grey along from the start. His anxieties proved groundless, as Desert Orchid again jauntily demonstrated his unrivalled versatility. Two miles or three miles five furlongs now came alike to this most remarkable of chasers.

As Desert Orchid roared away in the lead, the 2–1 favourite Vodkatini, perhaps sensing an impossible battle ahead, dug in his toes and refused to start. The others tried to chase the bobbing grey backside far ahead but you might as well try to catch Concorde in a flying boat. Desert Orchid, imperious as ever at Sandown, won, easing up, by twelve lengths and as he jig-jogged back along the rhododendron walk an army of supporters rushed from the stands to salute him in the unsaddling enclosure.

It was his twenty-third victory in fifty races and took his tally of first-prize money well past £200,000. Simon Sherwood was now unbeaten on him in five races. The jockey gasped, 'This must be the best chaser for at least twenty years. You just know he's always going to run his heart out for you.'

Afterwards, for the first time, came a hint that Desert Orchid

'Well done old pal,' says Colin Brown to his long-time partner

might, after all, be aimed at the Cheltenham Gold Cup. David Elsworth confirmed: 'His popularity is such that everyone wants to see him run in the Gold Cup and that includes myself and Richard.'

Simon Sherwood was in the wars again the following week after another fall at Huntingdon and this time his injuries were even more serious. He tried to drive home but was in such pain he was taken to Swindon Hospital where severe abdominal damage was diagnosed. Constant blood transfusions were needed to deal with internal bleeding and the massive bruising on his stomach even reached vital parts that had never been black before. Surgeons told him they did not understand how his pelvis had not been broken in the fall.

As soon as he could walk he began extensive physiotherapy treatment under the guidance of John Skull, a former professional footballer, who has helped so many jockeys overcome their injuries with unnatural speed. Certainly no jockey could ask for a better incentive to defy nature than the chance to ride Desert Orchid in the King George VI Rank Chase at Kempton on Boxing Day. Swimming sessions at a hydrotherapy pool in

Mrs Midge Burridge, who now runs the Desert Orchid fan club, discusses arrangements with the grey

Swindon, walking, jogging and daily treatment from John Skull all played their part in overcoming the dire effects of the original haemorrhage. Such was Simon Sherwood's recovery that he decided to ride in all three races before the main event of the day.

He was relieved to finish safely in all three and had the most comfortable possible ride on Desert Orchid in the circumstances. This time Desert Orchid did not go off at the lunatic pace of the previous year and Vodkatini even led for a spell in the middle of the race. But the grey was in command on the final turn, popped neatly over the three remaining fences and strolled up to the winning post with deceptive casualness.

Richard Burridge had spent the night before the big race sleeping in his car with his dogs outside Desert Orchid's box at Whitsbury. It was not perhaps the ideal way to end the Christmas festivities but the presence of the owner and his dogs would certainly have deterred any intruders with malicious intent.

Desert Orchid's ante-post price for the Gold Cup shortened further to 5–1 after Kempton but we would have to wait a further two months before learning if he would take his chance at Cheltenham.

By now Desert Orchid had undoubtedly become the most popular steeplechaser since Arkle, a horse who also possessed an unerring ability to lift our hearts and brighten our lives immeasurably. He was defeated only four times in twenty-six steeplechases, won three consecutive Gold Cups and in one of his defeats failed, if that is the correct phrase, by a nail-biting half length to give the grey, Stalbridge Colonist, 35 pounds in the 1966 Hennessy Gold Cup. The previous season Stalbridge Colonist had won eleven of his fourteen races.

Simon Sherwood was far too young to see Arkle in action, but he remembers his father talking reverently about the great horse and is understandably wary of being drawn into comparisons. But he is willing, indeed anxious, to declare his boundless praise of Desert Orchid.

Simon insists, 'He is the most complete horse I've ever ridden, so versatile he dominates at all distances from two miles to three and a half miles plus. Perhaps it would be blasphemous for me to compare him with Arkle. But simply on what he has achieved he must rate as one of the all-time greats. I've never known anything like him.'

There was a further chance to marvel at Desert Orchid's versatility in the Victor Chandler Handicap Chase over two miles at Ascot on 14 January. This time the handicapper appeared to have set the grey an impossible task, but the concession of lumps of weight to the best handicappers in training no longer seemed to inconvenience him. How we cheered at Ascot as he fought back from certain defeat to snatch victory from Panto Prince on the very line. The distinctly different colours of the two brave horses made this finish a moment of great beauty as they approached the winning post locked together, the lean, jet black, glistening Prince on the far side and the imperious grey, almost white, champion tantalisingly close beside him.

Brendan Powell still does not understand how he was caught after taking a decisive lead on Panto Prince, who was receiving 22 pounds, early in the straight.

Shaking his head in wonder, Brendan explains, 'Desert Orchid was well beaten at the second last and we won the race everywhere except where it matters. I can't believe what happened. The grey must have a heart as big as himself. Twenty-five yards from the post I felt him coming across ever nearer to me until his head was virtually touching my knee. The trouble is the closer he gets to you the more he fights.'

One of David Elsworth's prizes for being leading trainer at Liverpool the previous April was a return flight for two to Australia. Trainers who mix flat racing with jumping have precious little time for holidays, but Elsworth had been talking about taking Jane away for a mid-winter break for years and the tickets gave him the perfect excuse. He set off happily for a well-deserved holiday in the sunshine, leaving his team at home

BELOW & RIGHT: *Desert Orchid and Panto Prince are inseparable at the last fence in the Victor Chandler Handicap Chase at Ascot on 14 January*

Stride for stride the two combatants stretch for the winning post

Even the horse appears to be smiling

in the capable care of Chris Hill, his most experienced assistant, and Rodney Boult. David Elsworth was in a hired camper somewhere in the outback when Desert Orchid ran next in the Gainsborough Handicap Chase at Sandown on 4 February, but though it was the middle of the night in Australia he found a telephone to hear reports of the grey.

The news was good, though for the second time running Desert Orchid had to call on his matchless reserves of courage to defy the handicapper. This time it was the hapless Pegwell Bay who was caught and passed in the last 50 yards by Desert

Another towering leap by Desert Orchid at his favourite course, Sandown, in the Gainsborough Chase

A worm's-eye view of the dashing grey at another Sandown fence

Orchid's furious and now familiar late rally. Pegwell Bay, a formidable opponent, had been given an outstanding chance by the handicapper. Earlier in the season he had become the first horse to win Cheltenham's two major autumn prizes, the Mackeson Gold Cup and the A. F. Budge Gold Cup, in the same year. At Sandown Desert Orchid was required to give him 18 pounds, the equivalent of eighteen lengths. He did it, but only just. Certainly defeat appeared to come crowding in on Desert Orchid as Pegwell Bay stole a length's advantage after the final fence. But once again we were treated to a supreme example of the unquenchable will to win of this extraordinary steeplechaser, a horse of purity and such patent honesty. Grown men wept unashamedly as they rushed to acclaim him after this latest heart-stopping triumph and three cheers rang out stirringly for Desert Orchid as he returned to unsaddle.

When the excitement eventually died down, Simon Sherwood pointed out that all available evidence was surely in favour of allowing Desert Orchid to run in the Gold Cup, but even now Richard Burridge expressed his misgivings. He stated, 'The Gold Cup is an ugly race, so very tough that it exhausts horses. So many do not seem to recover from it. Desert Orchid's welfare is our first priority.'

Again Simon Sherwood was emphatic that Desert Orchid should go to Cheltenham and his comments gave an intriguing insight into the horse's personality.

'In a race with him everything revolves around his ears. You can always tell when he's a little bit in distress, because his old ears start coming back. When they flick back and forward you know he's enjoying himself. He has funny old quirks and is at

Desert Orchid and Pegwell Bay in glorious unison

LEFT & MIDDLE: *The pair are still together at the last and on the flat*

Every picture tells a story. There's only one winner now

his worst going to the start, sometimes a real horror because he is so very strong. But in a race he's one of the easiest horses of all for a jockey. If I knew I was going to ride Desert Orchid every Saturday through the season, I would not bother with midweek racing.'

Desert Orchid was by now, quite clearly, head and shoulders above any other chaser in the country. Early in March David Elsworth and the grey's owners announced that he would, after all, go for the Gold Cup at Cheltenham. It was the only possible decision and the one for which nearly everyone in racing had been hoping.

Elsworth commented, 'He is the best horse in the country by far. He has to run.'

But even he cannot have suspected what drama and emotion lay ahead.

CHAPTER TWELVE

The Desert Orchid fan club

Security was an extra worry in the days before Cheltenham. A year earlier Playschool, the favourite for the Gold Cup, arrived at the start panting heavily like a dog, ran lifelessly and was pulled up almost a mile from home. His trainer David Barons remains convinced he was doped in the final hours before the Gold Cup, though a major Jockey Club investigation failed to find any evidence of malpractice.

A security firm was brought in to protect Desert Orchid at Whitsbury in the build-up to Cheltenham. He was guarded, too, at the racecourse and even when he left the paddock for the long walk out onto the course he was surrounded by the foursome of Janice Coyle, Peter Maughan, Richard Burridge and his brother to ensure that straying hands could not harm him.

Desert Orchid's races have always been a marvellous excuse for the gathering of the Burridge clans. Wives, girlfriends and other members of the family have all had untold enjoyment from his exploits. James Burridge's second wife Midge is a great supporter, and invariably his first wife Ann will also come along to cheer the horse. Richard's two brothers, the twins Johnny and Simon, are most loyal followers too.

Janice Coyle was among those who wondered if Desert Orchid should run in the Gold Cup. Her fears were understandable following the tragic death on the opening day of the meeting of Chesham Squire, a horse she rode regularly at home. It is history now that those anxieties, shared by a number of the grey's faithful band of admirers, were swept aside in the most valiant manner.

The Elsworths and Burridges were inundated with cards, letters and presents for Desert Orchid in the aftermath of Cheltenham. The unprecedented scale of interest was such that Richard Burridge decided to introduce an official fan club for jump racing's outstanding celebrity to cope with requests for photographs and mementos of his races, including shoes and

Moments before disaster at Liverpool, Desert Orchid leads over the water

The fall at Liverpool that we thought would never happen. Desert Orchid gets much too close to the fence and pays the penalty. Charter Party blunders too and his jockey Richard Dunwoody joins Desert Orchid and Simon Sherwood in a tangled heap as Delius gallops past (Kenneth Bright)

even hairs from his tail. It was made clear that the enterprise would not be for profit and that any revenue would pass into a charitable fund.

A few of those who wrote after the Gold Cup expressed a desire for Desert Orchid to be retired. The response from owners and trainer was unanimous. The grey would continue in training for the very good reason that he loves to race and jump fences.

When the weights for the Whitbread Gold Cup were announced at the end of March a storm erupted around the ears of Christopher Mordaunt, the Jockey Club's senior handicapper for steeplechasing. Mr Mordaunt is, I know from personal experience, a kind and decent man, though you would not have guessed it from some of the vitriolic comments at his decision to give Desert Orchid top weight of 12 stone 2 pounds, fully 15 pounds more than Yahoo, the horse he beat so narrowly at Cheltenham.

David Elsworth expressed apprehension and Richard Burridge voiced disappointment at such a big weight. Others were much more free in their criticism and Desert Orchid's enormous popularity ensured that the arguments raged for days.

Christopher Mordaunt responded by explaining: 'My task was to try to strike a balance between giving Desert Orchid a fair weight while at the same time getting as many runners into the handicap as possible. At the moment he is rated 15 pounds or more superior to every other horse in training.

'He did after all win the race with 11 stone 11 pounds last year and he would certainly not be the first to carry more than 12 stone. I am not saying he is in Arkle's class but his supremacy over his current rivals is very marked indeed and I had to give him a weight compatible with that supremacy.'

Mordaunt's exercise was further complicated by one undeniable fact. Most jumpers reach a level of performance after three or four seasons and hold it for a while before their form begins to decline with age. Desert Orchid, remarkably, has continued to improve each year since he first came into training late in 1982. It is his present degree of excellence, his startling superiority allied to his invincible spirit that has made the handicapper's job such a difficult one.

Before a decision could be made about running in the Whitbread Gold Cup there was the more immediate matter of attempting to win at Liverpool for the second year running at the Seagram Grand National meeting. All the evidence suggested Desert Orchid had recovered very quickly from his hard race in the Gold Cup.

'He's like an athlete who has won an Olympic gold medal,' reported his proud trainer. 'He's very fit and soon bounced back. There are no visible signs that the race affected him adversely in any way. He's like a well-oiled machine.'

Such is the extent of public interest in this extraordinary grey that television cameras recorded lengthy footage of his overnight stay at Haydock Park on his way to Liverpool.

When he reached Aintree racecourse on the morning of

Having shaken off his jockey Desert Orchid shows how it should be done

Thursday, 6 April he was immediately the centre of an unpar-alleled amount of media attention, his every move followed by television, radio and dozens of photographers. Desert Orchid looked very much on his toes, almost too wound up, when he was saddled for the Martell Cup Chase in full view of a large and fascinated audience. Once he almost pushed Janice Coyle through a wooden partition. Next he forcefully barged Richard Burridge out of the way.

The weights for this race, unlike a handicap, favoured Desert Orchid immeasurably as he had to concede only 8 pounds to his rivals who included Yahoo and Charter Party, second and third at Cheltenham, and also Beau Ranger, pulled out of this race at the last moment twelve months earlier and winner in 1986 at 40–1. Desert Orchid, his mane plaited immaculately as usual, led the parade of runners past the stands where bookies had installed him, inevitably, as a warm favourite at 5–4. Bets of £2,000, £3,000, £5,000 and £12,000 suggested a depth of support on his handsome head that was not entirely due to sentiment, though his task was by no means an easy one on going that was once more soft.

Desert Orchid, naturally, set off in front and led for more than a circuit, closely pressed by Beau Ranger, Delius and Charter Party, but going out into the country for the final time Simon Sherwood was already experiencing a nagging sense of unease.

'It was just that he was not giving me quite the same feeling he had done at Cheltenham. Maybe he was a bit tired,' he affirmed later.

The first fence in the back straight comes as the runners stretch off the tight bend going away from the stands. Desert Orchid reached the fence perhaps half a length in front of Charter Party, ran perilously into the bottom of it, clipped it hard on the way up then fell dramatically and heavily, rolling over his stricken jockey before rising nimbly to his feet and setting off in pursuit of the field. Beside him Charter Party, too, blundered so badly that his jockey Richard Dunwoody was sent crashing to the ground. So the winners of the last two Gold Cups had been claimed as one by an apparently innocuous park fence. What a strange coincidence that Dawn Run, who had won the Gold Cup amid wild scenes in 1986, had come down at the very first fence in this race three years ago.

A heartfelt groan of surprise and dismay rose from the crowd when it became clear that Desert Orchid had, indeed, fallen. Once, as a novice, he had unseated his jockey at Ascot but this was the first time he had fallen in thirty-four races over fences.

Simon Sherwood lay prone for a few moments, more in

shock than pain, before being helped up. Far away Desert Orchid, apparently none the worse for his unscheduled tumble, skipped cheerfully over the next two fences. Seconds after Yahoo won the race, gaining deserved compensation for his defeat at Cheltenham, Desert Orchid cantered steadily past the packed enclosures, then slowed, allowing himself to be caught by an alert racegoer who quickly handed him over to Richard Burridge.

He hurdled the running rails skilfully in his concern to reach his horse. Close behind him Janice Coyle, Peter Maughan and David Elsworth rushed anxiously down the course where the horse was being swamped by an ever-growing band of cameramen. As the grey came back, mercifully unscathed, relieved racegoers stood in the rain applauding. It was a singular tribute that underlined his unique popularity. His fall, if anything, made him more lovable than ever. Playing safe has never been his style. Boldness has been a constant companion. Steeplechasing is not a business for faint hearts.

His trainer, once again exhibiting his instinctive understanding of his best horse's outstanding qualities, commented, 'He is so willing he gives you more than you should ever expect from any racehorse. But even *he* does not have a divine right to win all the time. If you are totally committed to taking on fences as he does every time you are going to get it wrong sometimes. The important thing is that he is all right.'

Liverpool was the only occasion that Simon Sherwood did not win on Desert Orchid in ten races. Less than a fortnight later the jockey, aged 31, announced that he would retire from riding within a few weeks. The news was not totally unexpected since he was already planning to build a new stable complex at East Ilsley near Newbury in time to start training there in 1990. He duly retired immediately on dismounting from his last winner, Knighton Lad, at Haydock on 1st May. His decision was certainly influenced by the knowledge that if he continued for one or two more seasons nothing could possibly match the splendour of Desert Orchid's magnificent triumph at Cheltenham.

When the time came for various judgements and awards at the end of the 1988–9 season Desert Orchid, predictably, swept the board. He was, quite simply, everyone's Horse of the Year. But his alarming experience at Liverpool effectively ended all debate about the Whitbread Gold Cup. He would not be going to Sandown. His next important engagement would be at home in Leicestershire relaxing in a paddock all summer with nothing more strenuous in mind than munching rich green grass.

There, for the moment, we will leave him, more a national institution than a racehorse. A romantic figure, proud, arrogant even, indomitable and utterly inspiring.

The grey returns unharmed led by a relieved Richard Burridge and Janice Coyle

Racing Record

1982/3

KEMPTON	21 January			Good

Walton Novices' Hurdle — 2 miles
Unplaced (behind when fell last)

WINCANTON	24 February			Good

Mere Maiden Hurdle (Div. 1) — 2 miles
Unplaced

SANDOWN	11 March			Good

Lilac Novices' Hurdle (Div. 2) — 2 miles — £1,265.20

Diamond Hunter	5–11–5	S. Smith Eccles	4–1	1
Desert Orchid	4–10–6	C. Brown	7–1	2
Emperor Charles	6–11–5	B. de Haan	15–2	3

16 RAN   DISTANCES: neck, 3l.   TRAINED: N. GASELEE

NEWBURY	25 March			Heavy

March Novices' Hurdle (Div. 2) — 2 miles 100 yds
Unplaced

1983/4

ASCOT	29 October			Firm

Haig Whisky Novices' Hurdle (Qualifier) — 2 miles — £1,931.60

Desert Orchid	4–10–10	C. Brown	11–8	1
Lucky Rascal	4–10–6	P. Double	5–4	2
Sammy Lux	5–10–10	Mr P. Schofield	13–2	3

5 RAN   DISTANCES: 20l, 15l.

ASCOT	18 November			Firm

Bingley Novices' Hurdle — 2 miles — £2,316.50

Desert Orchid	4–11–6	C. Brown	1–2 fav	1
Don Giovanni	4–11–6	J. Francome	7–4	2
Gillie's Prince	4–10–11	W. Morris	25–1	3

3 RAN   DISTANCES: 15l, 30l.

SANDOWN	2 December			Firm

December Novices' Hurdle		2 miles 5f 75 yds		£4,885.20
Catch Phrase	5–11–4	R. Rowe	9–4	1
Desert Orchid	4–11–3	C. Brown	5–6 fav	2
Flash Fred	6–11–4	J. Lovejoy	16–1	3

9 RAN DISTANCES: $\frac{3}{4}$l, 10l. TRAINED: J. T. GIFFORD

KEMPTON	26 December			Good

Foodbrokers Armour Novices' Hurdle		2 miles		£3,548.00
Desert Orchid	4–11–10	R. Linley	7–4 fav	1
I Haventalight	4–10–10	J. Francome	5–2	2
Derby Dilly	4–10–10	J.J. O'Neill	9–1	3

10 RAN DISTANCES: 15l, 1l.

SANDOWN	7 January			Good

Tolworth Hurdle		2 miles		£4,482.00
Desert Orchid	5–11–11	C. Brown	5–6 fav	1
I Haventalight	5–11–7	J. Francome	4–1	2
Horn of Plenty	5–11–7	H. Davies	50–1	3

6 RAN DISTANCES: 8l, 15l.

ASCOT	8 February			Good

Datchet Novices' Hurdle		2 miles		£2,977.20
Desert Orchid	5–11–11	C. Brown	11–10 fav	1
Hill's Pageant	5–11–1	K. Mooney	12–1	2
Brown Trix	6–11–5	J. Francome	7–1	3

10 RAN DISTANCES: 8l, 12l.

WINCANTON	23 February			Yielding

Kingwell Pattern Hurdle		2 miles		£6,059.20
Desert Orchid	5–11–2	C. Brown	2–1 fav	1
Stans Pride	7–10–11	R. Crank	3–1	2
Very Promising	6–11–12	B. de Haan	8–1	3

9 RAN DISTANCES: 4l, 12l.

CHELTENHAM	13 March			Good

Waterford Crystal Champion Hurdle 2 miles
Unplaced

1984/5

KEMPTON	20 October				Good
Captain Quist Hurdle		2 miles			£3,915.00
Ra Nova	5–11–10	M. Perrett		5–1	1
Janus	6–11–4	R. Rowe		14–1	2
Desert Orchid	5–11–10	C. Brown		2–1 fav	3

10 RAN   DISTANCES: $1\frac{1}{2}$l, 4 l.   TRAINED: MRS N. KENNEDY

ASCOT	15 December				Good to soft
H.S.S. Hire Shops Hurdle		2 miles			£4,819.10
See You Then	4–11–8	J. Francome		11–10	1
Joy Ride	4–10–8	S. Smith Eccles		8–1	2
Desert Orchid	5–11–8	C. Brown		5–1	3

5 RAN   DISTANCES: 2 l, 5 l.   TRAINED: N. J. HENDERSON

KEMPTON	26 December				Good to soft
Ladbroke Christmas Hurdle		2 miles			£15,572.00
Browne's Gazette	6–11–3	D. Browne		11–8	1
Desert Orchid	5–11–3	C. Brown		10–1	2
See You Then	4–11–3	J. Francome		2–1	3

7 RAN   DISTANCES: 15 l, 10 l.   TRAINED: MRS M. DICKINSON

LEOPARDSTOWN	12 January				Good
Irish Sweeps Handicap Hurdle		2 miles			
Unplaced					

SANDOWN	2 February				Soft
Oteley Hurdle		2 miles			£4,417.20
Desert Orchid	6–11–5	C. Brown		2–1 fav	1
Mr Moonraker	8–10–10	B. Powell		5–1	2
Infielder	6–10–11	J. Francome		10–1	3

8 RAN   DISTANCES: 10 l, $1\frac{1}{2}$l.

CHELTENHAM	12 March				Good
Waterford Crystal Champion Hurdle		2 miles			
Unplaced (pulled up)					

CHEPSTOW	8 April				Heavy
Blue Circle Welsh Champion Hurdle		2 miles			
Unplaced (pulled up)					

ASCOT	13 April			Good

Trillium Handicap Hurdle
Unplaced (fell)

2 miles

1985/6

KEMPTON	19 October			Firm

Captain Quist Hurdle
Unplaced (fell)

2 miles

DEVON & EXETER	1 November			Good to firm

Woolea Lambskin Products Ltd of Street Novices' Chase   2 miles 1 furlong   £1,607.60

Desert Orchid	6–11–0	C. Brown	4–5 fav	1
Charcoal Wally	6–11–7	R. Linley	6–5	2
Pridden Jimmy	6–11–0	B. Wright	33–1	3

5 RAN   DISTANCES: 25l, dist.

ASCOT	15 November			Firm

Hurst Park Novices' Chase   2 miles   £7,987.20

Desert Orchid	6–11–4	C. Brown	4–9 fav	1
Cocaine	7–11–4	C. Mann	9–2	2
Yacare	6–11–4	R. Rowe	7–1	3

4 RAN   DISTANCES: 12l, dist.

SANDOWN	30 November			Good

Henry VIII Novices' Chase   2 miles 18 yds   £3,759.00

Desert Orchid	6–11–4	C. Brown	4–11 fav	1
Taffy Jones	6–10–12	P. Barton	5–1	2
Evening Song	6–10–7	R. Goldstein	33–1	3

5 RAN   DISTANCES: 7l, 5l.

ASCOT	14 December			Good

Killiney Novices' Chase $2\frac{1}{2}$ miles   £5,638.50

Desert Orchid	6–11–11	C. Brown	5–4 fav	1
Evening Song	6–10–7	R. Goldstein	50–1	2
Play Boy	6–10–12	J. Duggan	3–1	3

6 RAN   DISTANCES: 20l, 4l.

ASCOT	10 January			Good to soft

Thunder & Lightning Novices' Chase — 2 miles
Unplaced (unseated rider)

SANDOWN	1 February			Soft, heavy patches

Scilly Isles Novices' Chase — 2 miles 18 yds — £7,680.00

Berlin	7–11–10	D. Browne	5–2	1
Desert Orchid	7–11–10	C. Brown	10–11 fav	2
Allten Glazed	9–11–5	G. Bradley	7–1	3

6 RAN   DISTANCES: $\frac{1}{2}$ l, 15 l.   TRAINED: N. A. GASELEE

CHELTENHAM	11 March			Good to soft

Arkle Challenge Trophy (Chase) — 2 miles — £21,215.00

Oregon Trail	6–11–8	R. J. Beggan	14–1	1
Charcoal Wally	7–11–8	B. Powell	11–1	2
Desert Orchid	7–11–8	C. Brown	11–2	3

14 RAN   DISTANCES: $\frac{3}{4}$ l, 8 l.   TRAINED: S. CHRISTIAN

SANDOWN	25 March			Good to soft

British Aerospace Rapier Novices' Chase — 2$\frac{1}{2}$ miles 68 yds — £3,993.00

Clara Mountain	7–11–8	H. Davies	2–1	1
Desert Orchid	7–11–8	C. Brown	10–11 fav	2
Whiskey Eyes	5–10–9	M. Harrington	5–1	3

6 RAN   DISTANCES: 1$\frac{1}{2}$ l, 15 l.   TRAINED: CAPTAIN T. A. FORSTER

ASCOT	12 April			Good

Contiboard Novices' Handicap Chase — 2$\frac{1}{2}$ miles
Unplaced (fifth)

1986/7

SANDOWN	1 November			Good

Holsten Export Lager Handicap Chase — 2$\frac{1}{2}$ miles 68 yds — £4,950.20

Desert Orchid	7–10–3	C. Brown	7–4 jt fav	1
The Argonaut	8–10–0	S. Shilston	9–4	2
Very Promising	8–12–0	R. Dunwoody	7–4 jt fav	3

4 RAN   DISTANCES: 4 l, 3 l.

ASCOT	15 November			Good

H & T Walker Goddess Handicap Chase $2\frac{1}{2}$ miles
Unplaced (fourth of six)

ASCOT	13 December			Good

Frogmore Handicap Chase   2 miles   £6,801.30

Desert Orchid	7–11–5	C. Brown	7–2 jt fav	1
Charcoal Wally	7–11–3	B. Powell	4–1	2
Little Bay	11–11–10	P. Tuck	7–2 jt fav	3

8 RAN   DISTANCES: 12l, $2\frac{1}{2}$l.

KEMPTON	26 December			Soft

King George VI Rank Chase   3 miles   £31,696.00

Desert Orchid	7–11–10	S. Sherwood	16–1	1
Door Latch	8–11–10	R. Rowe	10–1	2
Bolands Cross	7–11–10	P. Scudamore	9–2	3

9 RAN   DISTANCES: 15l, 6l.

SANDOWN	7 February			Good

F.U.'s Jeans Gainsborough Handicap Chase   3 miles 118 yds   £15,666.00

Desert Orchid	8–11–10	C. Brown	11–4	1
Stearsby	8–11–4	G. McCourt	3–1	2
Bolands Cross	8–11–0	P. Scudamore	9–4 fav	3

6 RAN   DISTANCES: 10l, 3l.

WINCANTON	26 February			Good to soft

Jim Ford Challenge Cup   3 miles 1f   £6,322.90

Desert Orchid	8 11 11	C. Brown	1 2 fav	1
Mr Moonraker	10–11–7	B. Powell	4–1	2
Fire Drill	12–11–7	P. Richards	50–1	3

4 RAN   DISTANCES: 12l, dist.

CHELTENHAM	18 March			Good

Queen Mother Champion Chase   2 miles   £25,775.00

Pearlyman	8–12–0	P. Scudamore	13–8	1
Very Promising	9–12–0	R. Dunwoody	3–1	2
Desert Orchid	8–12–0	C. Brown	9–4	3

8 RAN   DISTANCES: neck, 3l.   TRAINED: J. EDWARDS

ASCOT	8 April		Good to soft – soft patches
Peregrine Handicap Chase		$2\frac{1}{2}$ miles	£7,142.10
Desert Orchid	8–12–4	C. Brown	7–4 fav	1
Gold Bearer	7–9–10	G. Landau	33–1	2
Sign Again	9–10–3	R. Dunwoody	10–1	3

7 RAN   DISTANCES: 2l, 3l.

SANDOWN	25 April		Firm
Whitbread Gold Cup		3 miles 5f 18 yds	
Unplaced (pulled up)			

1987/8

WINCANTON	29 October		Good
Terry Biddlecombe Challenge Trophy		2 miles 5f	£3,842.00
Desert Orchid	8–11–8	C. Brown	1–7 fav	1
Sugar Bee	9–11–8	H. Davies	6–1	2
Britannicus	11–11–1	D. Morris	25–1	3

3 RAN   DISTANCES: dist., dist.

KEMPTON	18 November		Good to soft
Rank Boxing Day Trial Chase		$2\frac{1}{2}$ miles	£7,502.50
Desert Orchid	8–11–10	C. Brown	1–5 fav	1
Bishops Yarn	8–10–10	R. Guest	7–1	2
Galway Blaze	11–10–10	S. Sherwood	8–1	3

3 RAN   DISTANCES: 12l, 1l.

SANDOWN	5 December		Good
Tingle Creek Handicap Chase		2 miles 18 yds	£8,796.25
Long Engagement	6–10–2	R. Dunwoody	3–1	1
Desert Orchid	8–12–0	C. Brown	10–11	2
Amber Rambler	8–9–10	B. Walsh	5–1	3

5 RAN   DISTANCES: 3l, 15l.   TRAINED: D. NICHOLSON

KEMPTON	26 December		Good
King George VI Rank Chase		3 miles	£31,400.00
Nupsala (FR)	8–11–10	A. Pommier	25–1	1
Desert Orchid	8–11–10	C. Brown	Evens fav	2
Golden Friend	9–11–10	D. Browne	20–1	3

9 RAN   DISTANCES: 15l, 3l.   TRAINED: F. DOUMEN, FRANCE

SANDOWN — 6 February — Heavy

Lee Cooper Gainsborough Handicap Chase — 3 miles 118 yds — £20,450.00

Charter Party	10–10–11	R. Dunwoody	100–30 fav	1
Rhyme 'n' Reason	9–10–7	B. Powell	7–2	2
Desert Orchid	9–12–0	C. Brown	7–2	3

11 RAN   DISTANCES: 8l, neck.   TRAINED: D. NICHOLSON

WINCANTON — 25 February — Good to soft

Jim Ford Challenge Cup — 3 miles 1f — £7,572.00

Kildimo	8–11–11	G. Bradley	2–1	1
Desert Orchid	9–11–11	C. Brown	1–2 fav	2
Burrough Hill Lad	12–11–11	R. Rowe	9–1	3

3 RAN   DISTANCES: 1½l, dist.   TRAINED: G. B. BALDING

CHELTENHAM — 16 March — Heavy

Queen Mother Champion Chase — 2 miles — £39,836.00

Pearlyman	9–12–0	T. Morgan	15–8 fav	1
Desert Orchid	9–12–0	C. Brown	9–1	2
Very Promising	10–12–0	R. Dunwoody	4–1	3

8 RAN   DISTANCES: 5l, 1l.   TRAINED: J. EDWARDS

LIVERPOOL — 7 April — Good

Chivas Regal Cup — 3 miles 1f — £16,040.00

Desert Orchid	9–11–5	S. Sherwood	3–1	1
Kildimo	8–11–5	G. Bradley	2–1 fav	2
Weather the Storm	8–11–13	T. J. Taaffe	8–1	3

4 RAN   DISTANCES: 8l, 12l.

SANDOWN — 23 April — Good to firm

Whitbread Gold Cup — 3 miles 5f 18 yds — £45,000.00

Desert Orchid	9–11–11	S. Sherwood	6–1	1
Kildimo	8–11–12	J. Frost	6–1	2
Strands of Gold	9–10–0	P. Scudamore	6–1	3

12 RAN   DISTANCES: 2½l, 4l.

1988/9

WINCANTON	27 October			Good
Terry Biddlecombe Challenge Trophy	2 miles 5f			£3,694.00
Desert Orchid	9–11–8	S. Sherwood	2–7 fav	1
Biships Yarn	9–11–8	R. Guest	9–1	2
Golden Friend	10–11–8	D. Browne	5–1	3

5 RAN   DISTANCES: 15 l, ½ l.

SANDOWN	3 December			Good
Tingle Creek Handicap Chase	2 miles 18 yds			£8,812.50
Desert Orchid	9–12–0	S. Sherwood	5–2	1
Jim Thorpe	7–10–8	M. Dwyer	3–1	2
Panto Prince	7–10–10	B. Powell	4–1	3

5 RAN   DISTANCES: 12 l, ½ l.

KEMPTON	26 December			Good to firm
King George VI Rank Chase	3 miles			£37,280.00
Desert Orchid	9–11–10	S. Sherwood	1–2 fav	1
Kildimo	8–11–10	J. Frost	8–1	2
Vodkatini	9–11–10	Peter Hobbs	7–1	3

5 RAN   DISTANCES: 4 l, 5 l.

ASCOT	14 January			Good
Victor Chandler Handicap Chase	2 miles			£21,949.50
Desert Orchid	10–12–0	S. Sherwood	6–4 fav	1
Panto Prince	8–10–6	B. Powell	3–1	2
Ida's Delight	10–10–0	P. Dennis	66–1	3

5 RAN   DISTANCES: head, 8 l.

SANDOWN	4 February			Good
Racecall Gainsborough Handicap Chase	3 miles 118 yds			£19,340.00
Desert Orchid	10–12–0	S. Sherwood	6–5 fav	1
Pegwell Bay	8–10–10	C. Llewellyn	4–1	2
Kildimo	9–10–13	J. Frost	2–1	3

4 RAN   DISTANCES: ¾ l, 2½ l.

CHELTENHAM	16 March				Heavy

Tote Cheltenham Gold Cup		$3\frac{1}{4}$ miles			£68,371.25
Desert Orchid	10–12–0	S. Sherwood		5–2 fav	1
Yahoo	8–12–0	T. Morgan		25–1	2
Charter Party	11–12–0	R. Dunwoody		14–1	3

13 RAN DISTANCES: $1\frac{1}{2}$l, 8l.

LIVERPOOL	6 April		Soft

Martell Cup Chase 3 miles 1f
Unplaced (fell)

TOTAL FIRST PRIZE MONEY WON: £349,134.25

Flat Record

1985

ASCOT	1 May		Good

Mono Sagaro Stakes 2 miles
Unplaced